MANAGING BY THE NUMBERS

MANAGING BY THE NUMBERS

A Commonsense Guide to Understanding and Using Your Company's Financials

An Essential Resource for Growing Businesses

CHUCK KREMER
RON RIZZUTO
with JOHN CASE

Developed in Partnership with **Inc.**

PERSEUS PUBLISHING
Cambridge, Massachusetts

Many of the designations used by manufacturers and sellers to distinguish their products are claimed as trademarks. Where those designations appear in this book and when Perseus Publishing was aware of a trademark claim, the designations have been printed in initial capital letters.

A CIP record for this book is available from the Library of Congress.
ISBN: 0-7382-0256-8
Copyright © 2000 Chuck Kremer, Ron Rizzuto, and John Case

The Mobley Matrix©, referred to in this text as the Financial Scoreboard©, is protected by a compilation copyright jointly owned by Chris Mobley, Mobley Matrix International, Inc., and Chuck Kremer. The use in this book of the Mobley Matrix is in no way a waiver of the owners' compilation (software development) copyright property rights in the material. If you would like information on obtaining the rights for use of the Financial Scoreboard for software development, contact Chuck Kremer by phone at 303-986-8889, or by e-mail at chuck_busliteracy@compuserve.com.

Perseus Publishing is a member of the Perseus Books Group.

Text design by Cynthia Young
Set in 12-point Adobe Garamond by the Perseus Books Group

1 2 3 4 5 6 7 8 9 10—03 02 01 00
First printing, March 2000

Perseus Publishing books are available at special discounts for bulk purchases in the U.S. by corporations, institutions, and other organizations. For more information, please contact the Special Markets Department at HarperCollins Publishers, 10 East 53rd Street, New York, NY 10022, or call 1-212-207-7528.

Find us on the World Wide Web at http://www.perseuspublishing.com

CONTENTS

Part 3
Financial Analysis to Boost Performance

TABLES AND GRAPHS

GRAPHS

ACKNOWLEDGMENTS

The authors wish to thank the following people for their help, inspiration, and support in the preparation of this book: Bob Block, Eli Goldratt, Karen Kalkbrenner, Kate McKeown, Chris Mobley, Judith Orloff, Jack Stack, and the late Lou Mobley.

INTRODUCTION

What You'll Learn from This Book

Just to make sure this is the right book for you, we want to ask you a few questions:

- Do you get *complete* financial reports on your business at least every month?
- Do you *understand* what all those numbers mean? If you ask your accountant to explain them, can you make sense of what he or she tells you?
- Most important, do you *use* the information in those reports to help you make smart decisions about your business?

If the answer to any one of these questions is no, don't be alarmed: you're in good company. We bet that 50 percent of small-company owners and managers don't get complete, timely information about their business's financial performance. We also bet that fully 90 percent don't really understand or use the information they do see.

This should come as no surprise. After all, not many people who start or run their own business are trained in accounting or financial analysis. Sure, maybe you took a course or two in school—but how much do you really remember? Since we teach finance for a living, we'd like to think that our students treasure every word and remember every concept all their lives. Reality, alas, doesn't always live up to our hopes.

Anyway, if you answered no to any of our three questions, this is the book for you. It will teach you what complete financial reports are and how to understand them. It will show you how to use the information to run a better, more profitable company.

Do you really need to know this stuff? We think you do, but not because we believe that every businessperson should be a bean counter. Rather, it's because running a company is hard. You need every tool at your disposal, and good financial information is an extremely powerful tool.

Maybe, for instance, you've found yourself in situations like these:

- You're working your tail off, and the company is growing. Your accountant tells you the company is profitable. ("Great bottom line last quarter, Tom.") But you're always scrambling to pay the bills because there's never any cash in the bank. How come?
- Business was great last year, and you want to expand into a new facility. But your banker takes one look at your financials and shakes her head. "You haven't got the cash flow to support the loan you're asking for," she says. You're puzzled—hasn't business been good?
- A new competitor opened up down the street and you're feeling the pinch. You know you have to make some cuts—but where? Which product lines are least profitable? If you let some people go, how much will you really save?

Financial information can help you solve these problems. It can also help you take advantage of opportunities. In fact, it can help you make many of the tough decisions that business owners and managers must make every day. You wouldn't fly a plane without all the dials and gauges that show you where you're headed and whether everything's working the way it's supposed to. Similarly, you really don't want to run a business without the reports and information that show you where you're on track, where you're not, and whether the company is really making money.

Having said that, we want to clarify a couple of things.

First, this isn't a book about accounting. We assume you know some of the basic terms of finance, such as *depreciation*, *profit*, and *assets*. (Appendix 3 in the back of the book provides a glossary if you're a little shaky on some of these terms.) But we don't assume you know how to debit one account and credit another, or how to calculate different methods of depreciation. What's more, we aren't going to teach you that stuff. People who run businesses don't need to be accountants. They only need to make sure that their accountants (and their accounting software) give them the information they need—and that they know what to do with it.

Second, what's in this book isn't just a few lessons in the basics of financial analysis, lessons that any old accountant or professor could teach you if he or she had the time.

Rather, this book presents a unique approach to understanding the financials of your business—an approach that's as simple and as powerful as anything we have come across in our many, many years of teaching and working with businesses.

- It shows why you need *three separate financial statements*—three bottom lines, in effect—if you want a complete evaluation of your business's performance. Even today, many managers and accounting professionals rely on only one or two.
- It shows *how all these financial statements fit together*, and it provides you with a handy tool that summarizes the three bottom lines at a glance. This tool was developed by a pioneering thinker at IBM, the late Lou Mobley, and has been incorporated into the Financial Game for Decision Making seminar, produced by Educational Discoveries, Inc.
- It explains *what drives the three bottom lines*—and shows you how to manage your business so as to optimize your company's performance on all three measures.
- It shows you *how to create plans* to realize your company's goals—plans that you can actually make happen because they're grounded in financial reality.

In short, this is a book not for students of accounting but for managers and company owners who need or want to know how their business is really doing. It's a book that will help *you* run *your* company better.

The plan of the book follows this simple outline:

- Part 1 is a quick review of the three basic financial statements. If you're pretty sure you know what these statements are and what they show, skim them or even skip ahead to Part 2. However, we urge you *not* to skip Chapter 4, on cash-flow statements, unless you're entirely clear on how cash-flow statements differ from income statements. That difference—and the importance of tracking cash flow directly—are two of the key lessons in this book.
- Part 2 explains why it's never enough to look at any of these statements in isolation. It shows how the three statements (and the three bottom lines) fit together. It explains the Financial Scoreboard, a tool that lets you see the big financial picture of your company at a glance.
- Part 3 puts all this knowledge to work. It looks at the key drivers of each bottom line, and what you have to do to optimize each one. It shows how to use *forward-looking* financial information, that is, plans and projections that indicate what must happen if your company is to reach its goals.

When you have finished this book, we want to hear from you, particularly if you still have questions. The book, after all, is only as good and as useful as you find it to be. If you read it and don't understand something, we want to know what it is. Here's how to get in touch with Chuck or Ron:

Chuck Kremer
8632 West Warren Drive
Lakewood, Colorado 80227
chuck_busliteracy@compuserve.com

Ron Rizzuto
5124 South Jamaica Way
Englewood, Colorado 80111
rrizzuto@du.edu

For a demonstration of software that allows you to create the Financial Scoreboard described in this book, you may visit *Inc.* magazine's web site at www.inc.com/incproducts. (Search under "Finance.") For additional information and resources on financial management for your growing business, visit www.inc.com, www.ediscoveriesinc.com, and www.provant.com.

MANAGING BY THE NUMBERS

PART ONE

All You Really Need to Know about Financial Statements

ONE

Two Words on Accounting

Why Your Company's Checkbook Doesn't Tell You Everything You Need to Know

WOULDN'T IT BE GREAT IF COMPANIES DIDN'T NEED accounting? Business owners would save money. They wouldn't have to listen to all that financial jargon (and feel dumb because they don't understand it). If you look at households, it's tempting to believe that accounting really is unnecessary. Households have money coming in and money going out, just like businesses. But most families don't need an accountant; they can tell how they're doing just by looking at their bank accounts, their outstanding loans, and a few other numbers. Can't a business be run out of a checkbook in much the same way?

Unfortunately, it can't. Well, it *can*—but that's a surefire path to trouble.

The fact is, we're not big believers in many conventional accounting practices. We think that most financial statements are too hard to understand. We think they don't tell you everything you need to know. In this book, ironically, we'll be emphasizing the importance of a direct cash-flow statement, which many accountants ignore—and which isn't so different from checkbook-style accounting.

But we don't want to throw out the baby with the bathwater. We believe that the underlying principles of accounting are sound. We think it's a mistake to run any business, no matter how small, out of a checkbook, as if it were a household. The reasons aren't hard to understand.

First, more people are likely to have claims on a business's money. You know that the money in your family's bank account is yours. Sure, there are claims on it—the mortgage has to be paid every month—but the claims aren't hard to keep track of. Money in your business's bank account, however, is likely to have many more claims on it. The bank that gave you a loan has a claim. So do the vendors who sold you goods and services, and the company that leases you your equipment. Your employees have to be paid at the end of the week or the end of the month. And don't forget Uncle Sam—every day a business operates, it is likely to incur a tax liability of some sort.

Just looking at your business's checkbook balance doesn't tell you about all these claims. How much of that money has to go to taxes? How much should you set aside for loan payments? Not many of us can keep track of all of a business's obligations in our heads.

Second, businesses rarely operate on an all-cash basis. If your family is like most, your home accounts are relatively simple. You get a paycheck. You spend cash at the grocery store or the gas station. You pay your bills. At the end of each month, you have a pretty good idea of how you're doing (provided you're not strung out on credit cards!). With a business it isn't so easy. Most business transactions consist of a *sale*—essentially a promise or agreement—and a later *settlement*, which is when the money changes hands. Unless you keep track of both parts, you don't really know how you're doing.

To take a simple example, suppose you're a general contractor and you've just started a remodeling job. The customer has paid you 30 percent up front, so you have plenty of cash in the bank—but you haven't really earned that money yet. By the same token, when the job is nearing an end, you'll be in a different situation. You'll be out of pocket for your materials and labor, but you won't have collected that final payment from the customer. You'll have earned more than you have collected in cash.

Financial statements show both the *earned* part and the *cash* part. Or at least they should.

Third, businesses have to make more complex financial decisions. Most families' financial decisions aren't too complex. Families have to be sure their income covers their expenses, preferably with a little left over. They have to balance spending on current needs with saving for future needs. (That may be *hard* to do, but it isn't complex.) The people who own or run businesses face more complex decisions. They must decide when to invest in new equipment or a new location. They must figure out whether it's worthwhile to take out a loan or to hire another person. They must determine whether one line of business is as profitable as another. You simply can't make these decisions intelligently without good accounting information. That means you need a good accountant, good accounting software that you know how to use, or both.

Moreover, the value of a business in the long run depends on its financial performance. If your goal is to build up your business and keep it in good financial health so that you can eventually sell it or pass it on to your children, you *must* have a complete picture of how it is doing, month to month and year to year. Once again, you need the information that only an accounting system can provide.

If you're like a lot of business owners and managers, you've heard all this before. So what do you do?

Many business owners—particularly if they run one-person shops—just get a certified public accountant (CPA) to prepare their tax returns every year, figuring that the tax returns tell them how they're doing. Trouble is, a tax return may be the worst of all financial statements for running a company. You see it only once a year. It often contains both cash and noncash items (such as depreciation), and so it can leave you more confused than ever about whether you're really making money. In fact, good accountants will employ all sorts of perfectly legal techniques to *reduce* your bottom line on the tax return so as to minimize your current tax liability. The information you're required to provide the IRS is *not* the information you need to run the company effectively.

The next step beyond managing by tax return is obtaining (and looking at) monthly or quarterly financial statements. We hope you're already doing this because it's a great first step. But it is only a first step—and many accountants will tell you straight out that, yes indeed, you really do need more information than those statements typically provide. Also, as we said in the Introduction, not many businesspeople understand or make good use of the financial statements they do get. When it comes down to "believing" their financials or their company's checkbook, they go with the checkbook every time.

This is too bad because financial statements don't have to be as obscure or as hard to understand as they sometimes are. What's more, good financial reports show you what the money you have in your checkbook really means. They tell you important information such as

- how your company has performed financially over time
- whether you have a sufficient "cushion" against a business downturn
- how you stack up financially against competitors in your industry
- whether you have spent too much (or too little) on equipment
- how you're doing at collecting the money your customers owe you
- whether you'll be able to make payments on your outstanding loans
- whether you can afford to pay yourself more than you have in the past

along with the answers to many similar questions. It's all right there—in the balance sheet, the income statement, and the cash-flow statement. We'll take up these issues one at a time in the chapters that follow; we'll dissect them line by line and show you what each statement reveals about your business. Once that's done, we'll go on to discuss how the three financial statements fit together—and how you can use the information they provide to build a stronger, better-performing company.

TWO

The Balance Sheet

What a Company Owns and What It Owes

Ever notice something about a balance sheet? It has a date at the top. Not a span of time, just one day. It's usually the end of a year or quarter, but it can be the end of a month or any other date. What the balance sheet gives you is a snapshot of certain key facts about a business as of that date.

The word *snapshot* is important because the other financial statements we'll describe are different. They cover a period of time and show how your company did over that period of time. The balance sheet, by contrast, tells you how you ended up—or where you are right now. (For this reason the balance sheet is sometimes called the statement of financial position.)

And what does it show? The balance sheet all by itself tells you some interesting and important facts about your company:

- Is the business solvent—that is, are its assets at least equal to its liabilities? If the company were liquidated tomorrow, would the owners have anything to show for their effort? The balance sheet doesn't give you an ironclad answer to this question, for reasons we'll discuss below. But it gives you a rough indication of where you stand on this score.

- Is the business sufficiently liquid—that is, does it have enough cash and other liquid assets to cover its short-term obligations? In other words, are you going to be able to pay your bills during the period of time immediately following the date on the balance sheet?
- What do the company's assets consist of? A balance sheet shows you how much money you have in cash or short-term investments. It shows you how much you have tied up in inventory, and in plant and equipment. It also shows you how much you're owed by other people.
- Who has a claim on those assets? A balance sheet doesn't name names, of course. But it does show you how much you owe to various categories of creditors—vendors, lenders, the government, etc.—and how much belongs to the owners of the business.

There's a lot more you want to know about a company's financial situation and performance. That's why accountants invented the other statements we'll be discussing and why it's always a good idea to look at balance sheets from at least two periods, so you can see how the numbers you're interested in have changed over time. But for the moment, we'll focus on the terms and format of a single balance sheet. We'll illustrate the lesson—as we will throughout the book—with numbers belonging to a company we'll call SOHO Equipment, Inc. SOHO Equipment's name and financial statements are fictitious. But SOHO is modeled after a real business, and it's a lot like many, many small companies throughout the United States.

SOHO EQUIPMENT, INC.

It's September 1, and a couple named Bill and Carolyn Michaels are happy indeed. They have just taken what they think of as the second biggest step of their life. Two years earlier they had gotten married (that was number one on the list). Today, they are owners of their own business.

Kyle Williams is pretty happy too. He's the guy who sold them the business—and he's delighted to be out from under it.

The story goes back a few years. That was when Williams, who had worked in the office equipment industry for most of his career, began noticing a couple of interesting phenomena. One was the growing number of people working at home—"soloists," as they were coming to be known. Of course, many tradespeople and other self-employed folks had always worked out of their homes. But the new soloists were a much larger and more diverse group than before. They were sales representatives, computer programmers, and consultants. They were engineers, marketing specialists, and would-be entrepreneurs. Though most of the soloists worked alone, a few had two or three associates camped out in a den or spare bedroom. And though most were self-employed, a significant number were telecommuters.

Whatever their situation, Williams noted, the new soloists all had home offices, and the offices needed a lot of equipment. Each office had to have at least one computer and printer. It had to have telephone equipment, some kind of answering system, and a fax. Many of the offices needed a small copier. The soloists themselves needed laptops and cell phones for the time they spent on the road.

In short, the soloists as a group made up a large and growing market for office equipment. But Williams knew from experience that these people weren't buying from traditional office equipment companies like those he had worked for. Instead, they bought their equipment from mail-order suppliers or from the big office discount chains. He also knew from conversations with friends and business acquaintances who were setting up home offices that they weren't happy with their choices. They rarely knew what kind of equipment they needed. They didn't know what brands to buy. Computers in particular left most of them perplexed—all that talk in the ads about gigabytes, RAM, and megahertz just didn't make much sense. What's more, the soloists didn't trust the vendors they were dealing with to give them expert, impartial advice. When something went wrong with a piece of equipment—or when they found they needed something other than what they had bought—they had no one to call.

So Williams quit his job and started a new company, which he dubbed Williams Office Equipment. His business plan was simple. He would focus on people with home offices. He would offer them a limited but varied selection of high-quality equipment. He would help them understand exactly what they needed and customize their equipment as necessary. He would even offer "turnkey" services, going into a customer's home and setting up an office from scratch. If the equipment broke down or needed replacement, he would have service technicians on call. Williams figured that his hometown—a midsized Connecticut city—and its entire surrounding area were his marketplace. He cashed in some investments and refinanced his house. He bought inventory, rented a storefront, leased a van, hired a young man who had a way with computers, and took out a big ad in the local paper. He was in business.

But for Williams, the business was a disaster. Only a few years later, he was ready to get out.

He had been right about one thing: the company was a good idea. The market was definitely there. Soloists valued the services he offered, and many became customers. But the headaches! He hadn't realized how demanding customers could be—it seemed they were always calling with questions or problems, and Williams was a hands-on guy who wound up fielding most of the calls himself. He did manage to sell a fair amount of equipment. But his margins were poor; as a small dealer, he couldn't get great prices from the manufacturers, and he could never charge much more than the discount chain in the next town. Over time, he had accumulated a good deal of inventory, had bought three vans and a computer system, and had become known in the community. But he was still working seventy-hour weeks and barely scraping by.

The entrepreneurial life, he finally realized, just wasn't for him. When an old friend told him of a regional office equipment distributor that was looking for a vice president, Williams could scarcely get to the phone fast enough. It took him only a week to land the job. It took only another week to put Williams Equipment, Inc. up for sale.

This was the opportunity Bill and Carolyn Michaels—the buyers and new owners—had been looking for.

Both in their late thirties, Bill and Carolyn had met while working in the marketing department of a large company. But they didn't want to stay in their jobs, nor did they want to continue living in the big city where the company was located. Their ideal was to move to a smaller city, near their families, and to buy a business of their own. When a broker introduced them to Kyle Williams and Williams Equipment, they felt certain this was the company for them. It was in the right place. It was the right size. Thanks to an inheritance from Carolyn's uncle, they could afford it.

Of course, they did their due diligence. Bill inspected the inventory and pored over Kyle Williams's operations. Carolyn scouted out the competition and talked to some of the company's customers. They decided that the company had tremendous prospects for growth. Williams, they felt, had been too caught up in the day-to-day details to see the big picture. Always trying to do things himself, he couldn't offer first-rate service. Always desperate for cash, he required his customers to pay on delivery—and if they couldn't, he'd show up at their homes the next day seeking a check. (He had earned himself some ill will for this practice, Carolyn learned.)

Bill and Carolyn had big plans. They were both experienced marketers, and they were certain they could broaden the company's customer base considerably. They were also confident of their ability to attract and manage good people. They would advertise next-day delivery and world-class service. They would train their employees to provide what they were promising. They would also give their soloist customers thirty days to pay, just like "regular" businesses.

Like many buyers of small companies, Bill and Carolyn didn't actually purchase the stock of Williams Equipment, Inc. Instead, they set up a new corporation and acquired Williams Equipment's assets. (The transaction is known as an *asset sale*.) They even came up with a new name: SOHO Equipment, after the acronym for Small Office/Home Office, which was then catching on in the industry. One fine summer day, the deal was done and SOHO Equipment was in business. The company's balance sheet that day shows what the couple bought—and what their new company now owned.

UNDERSTANDING THE BALANCE SHEET: ASSETS

Thanks to accounting standards, every company in America has a balance sheet that follows a similar format. SOHO Equipment's may be a little simpler than General Electric's, but the categories and arrangement are similar. The first thing you'll see on any balance sheet—on the left-hand side, or on the top if the balance sheet is laid out vertically—is the heading *assets*.

"Assets" can be a difficult category to grasp because it includes different kinds of things. The cash a company has in the bank is an asset. So is the computer on the receptionist's desktop and the inventory in the warehouse. If customers owe the company money, the amount they owe is considered an asset. Assets are the things the company has and uses in its business that have value extending into the future. The assets side of the balance sheet shows what a business *owns*. Traditionally, they are listed in order of liquidity—that is, how easy it would be to turn them into cash.

So let's go down the asset categories one by one. First on the list comes *cash and cash equivalents*. This is real money. It includes what a company has in the bank. It also includes certificates of deposit (CDs) that mature in less than ninety days and shares in a money market fund. In most companies, cash is a small part of total assets—but it's the *only item anywhere on the balance sheet that you can actually spend right now*. Everything else on the assets side is either an item of value other than cash—a machine, say—or else an unsettled promise and agreement, such as a receivable. Kyle Williams had $25,000 in his company's checking account the day the company changed hands, and the buyers acquired that cash along with everything else.

Next on the list of assets comes *accounts receivable*. This is what people owe the business—that is, what they have promised to pay. Usually, most of the receivables consist of *trade receivables*, or what the company is owed by customers. Businesses expect to be paid by these customers in thirty days or so, so these receivables are almost like cash. Thanks to Kyle Williams's pay-on-demand policy, the new owners of SOHO Equipment have no receivables—though they will have some as soon as

TABLE 2.1   Balance Sheet, SOHO Equipment, Start-Up (assets only)

Assets	
Cash and cash equivalents	$25,000
Accounts receivable	0
Inventory	75,000
Notes receivable	0
Current assets	100,000
Gross fixed assets	100,000
Less accumulated depreciation	(0)
Net fixed assets	100,000
Goodwill, net	15,000
Other investments	0
Total assets	$215,000

NOTE: How to read a balance sheet—Balance sheets appear in a variety of formats. We use a common one here: some line items are subtotaled, and the subtotaling is indicated by a single line. For example, the first four line items in the statement above are subtotaled as current assets. Then all subtotals plus any items that are not included in a subtotal are added to get the total at the bottom. To get the $215,000 in total assets, for example, add the $100,000 in current assets, the $100,000 in net fixed assets, and the $15,000 in goodwill, net. Negative numbers in a balance sheet—numbers that must be subtracted when you're doing the totaling—are customarily indicated by parentheses. If there were any accumulated depreciation in the statement above, for instance, it would be subtracted from gross fixed assets to get net fixed assets.

they make their first credit sale. (Usually, the only companies with zero or near-zero receivables are retailers who don't offer their own charge cards to their customers.)

Then comes *inventory*. Companies in manufacturing industries have raw materials, work-in-process, and finished-goods inventory. Retailers and wholesalers have goods on the shelves waiting for sale. The inventory is valued according to various accounting principles relating to its cost. (Explaining these principles would take us beyond the scope of this book, but when you hear accountants argue about LIFO versus

FIFO, or last in first out versus first in first out, what they're discussing is different methods of valuing inventory.) The company hopes to sell this inventory before long, so it too is pretty close to cash. If you have more inventory than you can reasonably expect to sell quickly, however, you better not mentally count this as cash! Bill and Carolyn's new company acquired $75,000 worth of inventory in the transaction.

Next comes *notes receivable*. Notes receivable refers to interest-bearing loans the company has made, primarily to customers. SOHO has none, but many companies do.

The first several lines on the balance sheet—cash plus all the items that are expected to be converted to cash within twelve months—are summed up under the heading *current assets*. Then the balance sheet lists assets that are relatively illiquid—that is, assets that aren't expected to be converted into cash in that twelve-month period.

First in this category is an item we label *gross fixed assets*. (Many balance sheets label it *gross property, plant, and equipment*. Same thing.) This shows what a company has tied up in buildings, vehicles, machinery, and all the other tangible items a business buys and then expects to use over a long period of time. Most of the items in this category are very definitely *not* liquid: you wouldn't turn them into cash unless you decided to redeploy your assets—for example, by selling your building and leasing space instead. Bill and Carolyn's new company bought $100,000 worth of gross fixed assets, including Kyle Williams's vans and computer equipment.

Note a funny thing about that gross fixed assets number. When accountants write down the value of a company's fixed assets, they use what they call *historical cost*. In other words, they measure the value of an asset by what the business paid for it, not by what it may be worth now. This has implications that we'll explain in a moment.

Next comes an item called *accumulated depreciation*. Right here, unfortunately, is where some accountants and financial folks begin to confuse their clients. After all, almost everything else on the assets side of the balance sheet is something you can see, touch, collect, or spend. Accumulated depreciation, by contrast, is just some paper number. How can a business "own" accumulated depreciation?

The answer is, it doesn't. *Depreciation* is simply a way of spreading the cost of an asset over a certain number of years, with the time span roughly corresponding to the useful life of the asset. Accumulated depreciation is just a way of showing how much of the cost has been allocated to prior years.

An example should clarify this idea. Say you run a flower shop, and you bought a delivery truck three years ago for $25,000. The entire $25,000 is included in the gross fixed assets line of your balance sheet because that's what you paid for the truck (its historical cost). But by now, the truck is three years old, and its value has declined. Each year, your accountant has listed a portion of the truck's price as an expense on your income statement and is said to have *depreciated* it (more on this in the next chapter). The accumulated depreciation line on the balance sheet shows the total cumulative depreciation over the three years since you bought the truck.

So why is SOHO Equipment's accumulated depreciation zero? Simple: when business assets are sold to a new owner, their "fair" value is refigured as of the date of the sale. That becomes the new gross fixed assets figure, and the new owner begins depreciation all over again. When we see SOHO's balance sheet at the end of Bill and Carolyn's first year, we'll see some accumulated depreciation.

Typically, a balance sheet will then show *net fixed assets* or *net property, plant, and equipment,* which is just the gross number minus accumulated depreciation. The gross shows what the company paid for its fixed assets. The net shows that cost minus accumulated depreciation.

There may be other items on a balance sheet as well. *Other operating assets* is a catch-all category that can include items such as a prepaid insurance policy or prepaid rent on a building. (If other assets are short-term, they will appear above gross fixed assets; if they're long-term, they'll appear after net fixed assets.) *Other investments* refers to assets such as long-term CDs or equity in another business. And many companies, like SOHO Equipment, have a line labeled *goodwill.*

You're likely to run into this puzzling term *goodwill*—it's usually written as one word—any time a business is sold, and understanding it will help you understand the assets side of the balance sheet. All of the other assets on the balance sheet have a defined value. Cash and accounts receivable have a dollar value. So do fixed assets, with the dollar value determined as described earlier in this chapter. But someone who buys a company (even in an asset sale) is usually buying much more than just the assets recorded on the seller's balance sheet. The buyer gets an ongoing business. The company has a customer list, business relationships, a reputation, a place in the community. The price of the business will be determined not just by the value of the seller's assets but by the company's *market value*, which depends on these intangibles and many other factors that do not appear on the seller's balance sheet. What a buyer pays for a business is often more—sometimes much more—than the dollar value of the assets on the seller's balance sheet.

That "extra" that the buyer pays is what accountants call goodwill. It appears on the balance sheet just like any other asset, and it will be amortized over time much like any depreciable asset. It's the most common form of what are known as *intangible* assets—something that has value but can't be touched, collected, or spent. In this case, Bill and Carolyn paid $215,000 for the assets of Williams Equipment, Inc. Since the cash, inventory, and fixed assets were worth only $200,000, the remaining $15,000 is goodwill.

So that's it for assets. The last line on this section of the balance sheet is simply a summation of all the others. (Just be sure not to count both gross fixed assets and net fixed assets when you're adding.) For most small companies, the key items on the balance sheet are cash, accounts receivable, inventory (if the company has any), and net fixed assets. These items will nearly always show the bulk of what a business owns.

UNDERSTANDING THE BALANCE SHEET: LIABILITIES

Liabilities and equity make up the right-hand side (or the lower half) of a balance sheet. The liabilities entries show claims on the company's assets held by people outside the business. The equity entries show what's left for the company's owners after all the other claims have been accounted for.

TABLE 2.2   Balance Sheet, SOHO Equipment,
Start-Up (liabilities and equity only)

Liabilities	
Accounts payable	$ 0
Taxes payable	0
Other liabilities	0
Current liabilities	0
Long-term debt	10,000
Total liabilities	10,000
Equity	
Common stock	205,000
Retained earnings	0
Total equity	205,000
Total liabilities & equity	$215,000

What's on the list of a typical small company's liabilities? Liabilities are categorized by how current they are. Those that must be paid in the next twelve months are at the top, so we'll start there.

The first entry is *accounts payable*. That doesn't need much explanation: it's what a company owes its vendors and suppliers for goods and services purchased. SOHO Equipment doesn't have any payables at the time of the sale because outstanding bills are the responsibility of the seller. It will have some, of course, as soon as it begins to buy new inventory.

The next entry is *taxes payable*. Again, no explanation is necessary. What a company owes the government for income tax is just another kind of payable. And if the business has other short-term obligations, they'll be listed under *other liabilities*. This is another catch-all category: it might include vacation that employees have earned but haven't yet taken and deposits that the company has received from customers for work to be performed in the future. All the above liabilities are summed up under the heading *current liabilities*.

Then comes *long-term debt*. If your company has borrowed money from your uncle, the amount it owes will show up here. Bill and Carolyn Michaels negotiated a price with Kyle Williams, but they couldn't come up with the entire amount in cash. So Williams agreed to hold an interest-bearing note for $10,000, with the entire principal due in twenty-four months.

Most balance sheets then add up all these liabilities to show the company's *total liabilities*. Then come the entries that show *equity*. Typically, the equity entries are labeled *common stock* and/or *paid-in capital*, which includes all the money that shareholders have invested in the company, and *retained earnings*, which is all the accumulated profits the company has earned that it has never paid out to shareholders. Bill and Carolyn don't have any retained earnings yet, so their equity is wholly in the form of stock. The $205,000 represents the cash they themselves invested to buy stock in their new company.

UNDERSTANDING EQUITY
(AND WHY A BALANCE SHEET BALANCES)

Why does the balance sheet balance? And what do those "equity" entries mean, anyway? After all, equity isn't something the company owes anybody else. So why does it appear on the same side of the balance sheet as the "liabilities" entries, which show what the company owes?

The answers to these questions are related and are less puzzling than they may seem.

First, note an interesting fact about the balance sheet. The left side—the assets side—shows the money value of things. It shows cash in the bank, money that's owed the business, physical objects such as buildings and equipment, and intangible assets such as goodwill. The right side—the liabilities and equity side—is a little different. Sure, it's still numbers. But those numbers represent *people*. They represent liabilities the company has incurred to the people who are its creditors. They represent the value held by the people who own the business (equity). Lou Mobley of IBM liked to say that the balance sheet is a snapshot that connects things to people.

So equity is pretty simple—it's all the money that the company theoretically owes the owners of the business after everything it owes all creditors has been accounted for. Another way of saying it? Assets equal liabilities plus equity. (Accountants call this the *basic accounting equation.*)

So that's why the totals on both sides of a balance sheet are identical. It's why a balance sheet balances. Of course, accountants don't just subtract the liabilities from the assets and assume that whatever they get is the correct number for owners' equity. They have to add up common stock, paid-in capital and retained earnings, and be sure that the total *equals* assets minus liabilities. This can sometimes be a daunting task, which is why the world needs accountants after all.

It's also why equity appears on the "liabilities" side of the sheet. If you're a business owner, one thing you want to know from a balance sheet is, *how much do I* (or *we* or *the shareholders*) *have left over after we take into account everything that is owed to other people?* Add up the assets, subtract the liabilities, and presto: there's what your ownership in the business is worth, according to accounting rules.

Why did we put in that qualifier, "according to accounting rules"? Well, remember the explanation above: if you sell your stake in a business, it's going to be worth whatever someone wants to pay for it. What the balance sheet shows is *book value*—that is, what your assets minus your liabilities are worth according to historical cost, depreciation, and all the other rules accountants use to calculate their value.

As for Bill and Carolyn, they have invested $205,000 in a company that also has borrowed $10,000 from Kyle Williams, which right now is its only liability. It has $215,000 worth of assets. Its equity, or what the stockholders invested ($205,000), equals its assets ($215,000) minus its liabilities ($10,000).

TWO QUICK EXERCISES USING THE BALANCE SHEET

OK, enough on SOHO Equipment for the moment. Now we'd like you to get out your own company's last balance sheet and check it out. Look for two things.

First, is that equity figure a positive number? (We hope it is!) If it's a negative number, it's a sign that your company is in trouble or maybe just that it's new and struggling. Whatever the reason, right now you

TABLE 2.3   Balance Sheet, SOHO Equipment, Start-Up

Assets	
Cash and cash equivalents	$ 25,000
Accounts receivable	0
Inventory	75,000
Notes receivable	0
Current assets	100,000
Gross fixed assets	100,000
Less accumulated depreciation	(0)
Net fixed assets	100,000
Goodwill, net	15,000
Other investments	0
Total assets	$215,000
Liabilities and equity	
Accounts payable	$ 0
Taxes payable	0
Other liabilities	0
Current liabilities	0
Long-term debt	10,000
Total liabilities	10,000
Common stock	205,000
Retained earnings	0
Total equity	205,000
Total liabilities & equity	$215,000

don't have enough assets to cover your liabilities. You'll need a plan to change that situation as soon as possible.

Next, get out your calculator. Add the cash and accounts receivable figures on the assets side, and write down the sum. Separately, add accounts payable and any other current obligations listed on the liabilities side, and write down this sum. Then divide the first number by the second. What do you get? As a rule, the ratio should be greater than 1.00. If it isn't, it means you don't have enough cash and near cash to cover your short-term obligations (those due in the next twelve months). Ac-

TABLE 2.4   Quick and Current Ratios

$$\text{Quick Ratio} = \frac{\text{Cash} + \text{Accounts Receivable}}{\text{Accounts Payable} + \text{Other Current Liabilities}}$$

$$\text{Current Ratio} = \frac{\text{Cash} + \text{Accounts Receivable} + \text{Inventory} + \text{Other Current Assets}}{\text{Accounts Payable} + \text{Other Current Liabilities}}$$

countants call this the *quick ratio* or *acid test*. It's a useful tool for estimating at a glance whether your company is facing immediate liquidity problems. ("Liquidity problems" is accountant-ese for *not enough cash*.) However, it's only a first approximation. For one thing, you can have enough cash today and still run out of cash next month. For another, receivables are *not* always as good as cash; it depends on how old they are, and how confident you are of your ability to collect. We'll take up both these problems later in the book.

And please don't get the quick ratio confused with another tool, the *current ratio*. Your loan officer at the bank probably likes to look at the current ratio because it adds items such as inventory and other current assets into the cash and receivables figure and compares *that* total with short-term obligations. Loan officers figure that, in a pinch, they can always convert inventory into cash and get their money back. But to a manager, the current ratio can be misleading. If a company carries a lot of inventory, for instance, the current ratio looks better than if it carries only a little, all else being equal. However, carrying a lot of inventory isn't necessarily in a company's best interest.

Solvency and liquidity are just two of the items that financial people look at when they're assessing a company's balance sheet. You've probably heard these folks talk about "strong" and "weak" balance sheets. In general, a balance sheet is called strong when the company has a nice financial cushion. Its liabilities are small compared to its equity. A weak balance sheet is just the opposite: high liabilities compared to equity. Of course, this assessment of a balance sheet is never the whole picture of a business. As we'll see later on, a company can have more assets—even more cash—than it can profitably put to work. A large cash balance makes those current and quick ratios look good (again, all else being equal), but an astute analyst would want to know why that cash isn't being better reinvested. By the same token, a company with high liabilities relative to equity may be using borrowed money effectively to generate more profits than it otherwise could.

You also have to remember that the balance sheet is a snapshot, and to a certain extent the picture it portrays depends on when you snap the shutter. Say, for example, that your Uncle Harry owns a quarter of your company's stock and that you decide to use the company's unneeded cash to buy him out and retire the stock. The day *before* the transaction, your balance sheet shows all the cash you'll be using to buy his stock. The day *after* the transaction, the balance sheet shows a lot less cash (because it has been paid to Uncle Harry) and a lot less equity (because Uncle Harry's outstanding shares of stock have been reduced to zero), but just as many liabilities! The balance sheet is suddenly weaker because the company has less equity but no fewer liabilities, even though nothing else has changed in the business.

In sum, the balance sheet tells you some important information, like what the company owns and what it owes. But it also leaves out a lot. It doesn't tell you whether the company made money last year. It doesn't tell you where the company's cash came from and whether it has a healthy cash flow. That's why people invented other financial statements. We'll examine the two most important in the following chapters.

THREE

The Income Statement

What the P&L Tells You
(and What It Leaves Out)

THE SECOND IMPORTANT FINANCIAL REPORT IS CALLED THE income statement. It's also known as the statement of earnings, statement of operations, the profit-and-loss statement, or just the P&L. It shows you whether your company was profitable—whether it made money—over a given period or span of time.

Income statements are tremendously useful. They're also tremendously dangerous because they can be misleading. Looking only at your company's income statement, you can think that you have money to spend when you don't. You can think that everything in your business is healthy when some parts are not healthy at all.

To understand this danger, remember that most business transactions consist of two parts. First comes a promise and agreement. You agree to buy something from a vendor and you make a promise to pay. You agree to sell something to a customer and the customer promises to pay. Next comes the settlement, which is when the bills are paid and the cash actually changes hands. Virtually all businesses have these two-part transactions; even cash-based businesses like stores and restaurants don't usually pay their suppliers in cash.

Strange as it may sound, the income statement tracks *only* the promise and agreement part of a company's transactions. *It is not about cash.* It doesn't show the dollars coming in and out of your bank account. The number at the bottom of the income statement, net profit (or profit after tax), is not cash you can spend!

You might be asking, "If the income statement doesn't show me what I have to spend, what good is it?" In fact, the income statement is indispensable to a business. The reason is that it answers an important question—a question that runs something like this:

Let's take the value of all the goods or services we delivered during any given time period, whether or not we have been paid for them yet. Then let's figure out as accurately as we can what it cost us to provide those goods or services, regardless of whether we actually wrote checks for those costs. Now: are we making money from our delivery of those goods or services?

You can see that a good answer to this question would tell you a lot about how you're doing!

Naturally, accountants have had to come up with some clever ways of calculating costs. They have to take into account *all* of a company's costs, including overhead and the cost of borrowing and everything else, not just obvious items like wages and materials. At the same time, they can't just look in the checkbook to see what was spent because that wouldn't give an accurate picture.

So if you're a business owner, here's how they create your income statement.

First, when you provide goods or services to someone, either you get paid in cash or you count on being paid later, after you send the customer a bill. In either case, you record a sale. Accountants add up all these sales for a given time period and list them as sales (or revenue) on the top line of the income statement.

Next, they do their best to add up all the costs that are *connected* to those sales.

For example, say you run a clothing store. If your store buys several gross of golf shirts in March and sells them during April, May, and June, accountants don't count all the costs in March and all the revenue in April, May, and June. They count the cost of each shirt against the revenue from that shirt in the month that the shirt is sold.

And if you deliver your goods in a truck, they figure out how much you originally spent for the truck and how long it can be reasonably expected to last. Then they allocate a part of the total cost to the period of time covered by a particular income statement—a little bit for March, for April, for May, and so on.

Maybe you're familiar with the word *accrual*, as in "the accrual method of accounting." Most income statements are based on the principles of accrual. (We'll explain the exceptions in the following paragraph.) An accrual-based income statement shows sales over a given period of time (April, say) and the costs associated with April's sales, without reference to whether any cash has actually changed hands. It shows the revenues and costs that you have *accrued* in that time span. The beauty of such a statement is that it *matches* costs and expenses with the sales that took place during the time span it covers, and thereby lets you see if those sales are in fact making money. (Accountants refer to this as the *matching principle*.) If you were just looking at cash-in and cash-out, you wouldn't be able to tell what went with what.

What we have just said about income statements applies to all midsize and large companies. However, certain companies may choose to use something called a *cash-based income statement*. A cash-based income statement looks just like an accrual-based income statement, but it is compiled differently. Sales are recorded only when the cash is received. Costs are recorded when the checks are written. We don't recommend managing with a cash-based income statement even if you are allowed to file your taxes on this basis (see below). Yes, it's simple. Yes, it does let you postpone paying taxes on profits from sales you haven't yet collected. But it doesn't show you whether your company's sales are really profitable. And it doesn't even give you a complete picture of the cash flowing into and out of your company's bank account because some inflows and outflows of cash (for example, repayment of principal on a loan) are not recorded on an income statement.

Here's a quick summary of tax law as it relates to cash-based income statements. If a company has more than $5 million in sales, or has inventory, it is required by the IRS to use an accrual-based income statement for tax-reporting purposes. Other companies—that is, those with less than $5 million in sales and with no inventory—are allowed to report their taxes using cash-based income statements if they choose to do so initially. They may subsequently convert their tax returns from cash-based to accrual-based. Once they do that, however, they must stick to accrual; they're not allowed to convert back.

If your accountant tells you that you are eligible to file a cash-based tax return and advises you to do so, we urge you to do what many other small-business owners do. Use an accrual-based statement to manage your business. At year-end, ask the accountant to convert it to a cash-based statement *for tax purposes only*. The conversion isn't hard to do, and it will provide the tax advantage without depriving you of the information you get from an accrual-based statement.

At any rate, if a balance sheet is like a snapshot, an income statement is more like a movie: it tells what happened during a given a time span. Let's examine SOHO's income statement for its first year of operation.

SOHO EQUIPMENT: THE FIRST YEAR

When Bill and Carolyn set up their own company and bought out Williams Equipment, Inc., they were pretty excited. Bill's mother, a graphic designer, volunteered to develop a logo and then have stationery, business cards, and the like printed. The couple organized friends and family on a couple of fall weekends for cleanup and painting at the storefront. To Bill and Carolyn, it seemed that most of their regular work time that first month was spent on the phone. Bill called the reps who had handled the Williams Equipment account for a dozen different manufacturers and put out initial feelers to some other vendors. Carolyn methodically went down Williams's customer list, calling everyone who had bought from the company in the past four years and introducing herself. Part of every day was devoted—as it had been since the couple first got interested in the business—to a crash course in the office equipment industry. Both of the new owners were technologically savvy and knew a good deal about computers in particular. Still, they pored over catalogs, product literature, and trade magazines, educating themselves in the particulars of the business.

They also sat down with the employees they had "inherited" from Williams Equipment and talked about the future.

Kyle Williams had had three employees, all of whom wanted to stay. Charlie, a likable but awkward young man who loved computers, seemed to be able to customize a system in less time than it took him to eat lunch. Donna, thirty-something and recovering from a difficult marriage, seemed to like nothing so much as working. Claire, in her fifties, had returned to salaried work after raising a family and now spent four hours a day in the office. Donna and Charlie drove the vans and installed equipment, with Charlie doubling as computer technician and repair specialist. Claire managed the office, answered the phone, and dealt with walk-in customers. When the UPS truck arrived with a big delivery or when something else needed to be done, everyone helped out.

Talking with the employees, Bill and Carolyn explained their vision for SOHO Equipment. They emphasized the need for fast, high-quality service. They elaborated on what they saw as the possibilities for rapid growth. The company held opportunities for everybody, they said, if everyone pitched in and did whatever it took to keep customers happy.

It was only the fourth day of operation when Carolyn came out of her office grinning. She had made her first sale.

As she worked her way down the list of customers, she asked them if they needed anything right now. Bob Thomas, a sales rep for a regional air-handling equipment manufacturer who worked out of his home, did need something. His computer was three years old. He had read about some of the deals you could get on new computers these days from the discount stores, but he hadn't had time to look at them in person. Besides, he didn't like the idea of hooking it up himself. Though his friends all boasted that their twelve-year-olds could set up a computer, Bob's oldest child wasn't much help—he was only four.

Talking to Bob, Carolyn probed a little. Bob had some software from the company he represented that wouldn't work on his old computer. Yes, said Carolyn, SOHO could install that and get it up and running.

What else did he use the computer for? She ticked off a list of uses and explained to Bob that SOHO would install software for anything he needed. By the time she was through, she had sold not only a customized computer and some add-on software but a new printer as well. And yes: Charlie would be out to install it the next day.

As the first year wore on, sales mounted. Carolyn had a magic touch on the phone: customers liked her and wanted to buy from her. Bill cut deals with vendors to make sure the company always had plenty of inventory; he also mounted a direct-mail marketing campaign, targeting some 2,000 prospects in the area. Charlie and Donna seemed to work all the time, and even Claire, the part-timer, was enthusiastic about the new business. Over time, the new owners learned some interesting facts about the industry they were in. One was obvious: they could never come close to competing on price with the office discount houses, and Kyle Williams had been wrong even to think of himself in the same marketplace as the big chains. SOHO Equipment would never sell to soloists who needed rock-bottom prices and who were willing to do the work involved in setting up their offices.

On the other hand, the economy in that part of the country was booming. Many of Carolyn's prospective customers had more money than time—and they had no interest in shopping around for the best price on office equipment. On the contrary, they wanted someone to come in, do the work, and get everything up and running. They weren't really concerned with how much it all would cost. If SOHO could provide a full office setup—a customized computer, printer, high-tech telephone, fax, and all the necessary supplies—and if the system were all set up and ready to go, customers would pay top dollar. If they needed additional equipment such as scanners or copiers, so much the better.

It took Bill and Carolyn a few months to realize this, but as they did they slowly raised their prices. In January, SOHO recorded its best month ever: just over $80,000 in sales. In April they topped the record, hitting $85,000.

At the end of the fiscal year, the accountant they had hired closed the books. A few days later he presented Bill and Carolyn with their first year's income statement.

LINE ITEMS ON THE INCOME STATEMENT

Like balance sheets, income statements follow a more-or-less conventional format, so the income statement of SOHO Equipment is set up pretty much like every company's income statement. But "pretty much" does not mean "exactly." For one thing, there's no such thing as a sacred glossary for income statements. The terms we'll use here are among the most common, but many companies use different terminology. Then too, the categories themselves may vary just because types of business vary; what is a useful category for one business may not be useful to

TABLE 3.1 Income Statement, SOHO Equipment, Year 1

Sales	$500,000
Cost of goods sold	350,000
Gross profit	150,000
Depreciation	10,000
Goodwill amortization	1,000
Marketing & selling expense	25,000
General & administrative expense	130,000
Operating income	(16,000)
Interest and other expenses	1,000
Profit before taxes	(17,000)
Income taxes	0
Net profit	$(17,000)

NOTE: How to read an income statement—Like balance sheets, income statements reflect a series of subtotaling operations. In the format we use, the subtotals are indicated by a line. First, cost of goods sold is subtracted from sales to yield gross profit. Next, depreciation, goodwill amortization, and the lines immediately following are subtracted from gross profit to yield operating income. Then interest and other expense is subtracted to yield profit before taxes, and income taxes is subtracted to yield net profit. Negative totals are indicated by parentheses. In the example above, SOHO Equipment lost $17,000 in the first year, which shows up as a net profit of ($17,000).

another. You may want to get out your own company's income statement and see how it compares with SOHO Equipment's.

The first line on any income statement—the "top line"—is always *sales* or *revenue*. It's the dollar value of the goods or services that customers bought. Remember that on an accrual-based statement the sale doesn't have to be paid for to count as a sale. On the other hand, you can't ordinarily record a sale the instant that the customer places an order; you actually have to provide the goods or service. (For very long-running projects such as construction, revenue is sometimes recorded as the job reaches certain percentages of completion, instead of being recorded all at the end of the job. That's a topic beyond the scope of this book.)

Anyway, SOHO Equipment in its first year racked up $500,000 worth of sales. When they realized they had hit the half-million mark, Bill and Carolyn popped the cork on a bottle of champagne.

The next line for many companies is *cost of goods sold,* or COGS. COGS represents the cost to the company of all the goods that were provided during the period covered by the income statement. It's much the same as sales, except that sales shows the *price* the customer paid for the goods while COGS shows the *cost* of those same goods to the company.

What goes into COGS? It depends on the business and on the accounting practices followed. In a manufacturing company, COGS includes the cost of materials that go into making a product; the cost of the direct labor actually involved in producing the product; and a portion of "factory overhead," or all the expenses involved in running the factory that aren't tied directly to a single product. (Some companies refer to factory overhead as "burden.") For many manufacturers, COGS is the single most important number on the income statement because it is the biggest factor affecting profit. The same is true of some retailers and wholesalers, for whom COGS may be more than 90 percent of gross revenues. In those industries, COGS generally includes only the price of goods acquired for resale (plus, usually, "freight in"—that is, any shipping cost associated with getting the goods in stock).

Companies that don't deal in goods, of course, don't have a COGS line. Some service companies do have a line labeled COS, for *cost of sales* or *cost of services*, which represents the specific cost of providing services. For example, a seminar company might take all the costs associated with a particular seminar—the presenter's time and travel expenses, the cost of the room, instructional materials, and so forth—and consider those as COS. A consulting company might calculate COS for a particular project by adding up the direct labor (and materials, if any) related to the project.

In any event, note an important fact—one that escapes a lot of people who don't have financial training. COGS is *not* the same thing as what you might have added to your inventory during the period in question. To go back to that golf shirt example, COGS for the second quarter is the cost of all those shirts you shipped during April, May, and June. It doesn't include the back-to-school outfits that you bought in June but won't be selling until August. That cost doesn't appear on the income statement until the goods are sold.

SOHO Equipment registered $350,000 in COGS for its first year. This was the cost of all the equipment SOHO sold during the year.

Next on the income statement comes *gross profit*, which is just sales minus COGS or COS. Now and then you'll hear someone refer to this figure as "gross margin," but we think it's clearer if you call the dollar figure gross profit. Gross margin is better defined as a ratio: gross profit divided by sales. By this terminology, SOHO has a gross profit of $150,000 and a gross margin of 30 percent.

Depreciation (or "depreciation and amortization") is the next line on the income statement. This can get a little confusing, too.

As noted in the last chapter, companies buy many items that they expect to use for several years. Buildings and vehicles fall into this category. So does most machinery and much office equipment (including computer systems). Accountants *depreciate* these big-ticket items, which is to say they apportion the cost over their estimated useful life. The expense taken in any given year is called depreciation. Thus the florist who buys a delivery truck for $25,000 doesn't expense the total purchase in the year she bought the truck. Instead, her accountant will depreciate it over (say) five years, and a depreciation charge of $5,000 will show up on her annual income statement every year for five years.

Eventually, of course, the truck or any asset may be depreciated to zero—even though it's still in use.

You may also find the word *amortization* on your income statement. It's conceptually the same as depreciation, but it applies to intangible assets such as goodwill.

Here's another quirk of income statements: nearly every company has depreciable assets of some sort, but depreciation isn't always a separate line item on the statement. Manufacturing companies must include most of their depreciation in COGS. A training company might include depreciation in its overhead expense line, discussed below. None of this goes against accounting rules. However, we think that most companies should state depreciation separately. It helps you understand how the net book value of fixed assets on the balance sheet decreased. The new owners of SOHO, for example, bought $100,000 worth of fixed assets when they acquired the business. In the first year, Bill and Carolyn's accountant has depreciated those assets by 10 percent, or $10,000. The accountant has also amortized the goodwill acquired by Bill and Carolyn by $1,000. (That represents a decision by the owners and their accountant to amortize the goodwill over fifteen years, which is somewhat faster than required by accounting rules.)

The next lines on an income statement often vary. Some companies have one big heading: *marketing, selling, general and administrative expense*, or MSG&A. Other companies break out these expenses the way SOHO Equipment does, into *marketing and selling expenses* on the one hand and *general and administrative expenses* (G&A) on the other. There's no fixed rule; it depends on what makes the most sense for your business. Typically, selling costs include commissions to salespeople and may also include the cost of shipping goods to customers. Marketing costs include advertising, promotional programs, and so forth. General and administrative costs include office rent, office expenses, salaries of office personnel, and many other items that are sometimes called *nonmanufacturing overhead* or just *overhead*.

How important are the items that appear under MSG&A? Just as the terminology varies from one company to another, so does the importance of these items. For a large manufacturing business, most of the "action" will usually be in the COGS line, with MSG&A expenses just a small fraction of total costs. For a small service company, MSG&A is likely to be much more substantial. For SOHO, as you can see, the two lines that together make up MSG&A come to $155,000—or $5,000 more than the company's gross profit! That's not unusual in a small start-up situation like this one, but it's not something you'd like to see in most more mature businesses.

Incidentally, note that the difference between COGS and MSG&A is not quite the same as the distinction you may have learned in school between fixed and variable costs. Fixed costs are those that don't vary (in the short term) with the quantity of goods or services produced—for example, the cost of a building. Variable costs are those that do, such as the cost of materials in a product. COGS *is* mostly variable and MSG&A *is* mostly fixed, but there are plenty of exceptions. For example, COGS in manufacturing companies includes depreciation on machinery, which is a fixed cost. And selling expenses—part of MSG&A, however it is broken out—usually include sales commissions, which are variable.

The next line on SOHO Equipment's income statement is *operating income*, also called *operating profit*. You compute it by subtracting MSG&A expenses and depreciation and amortization from gross profit. Operating income can be another important number as well: if you're the business owner, it shows how much you are making from actually running your own business, omitting any cost of financing and any tax obligations you may incur. SOHO's operating income for the first year is a negative number: ($16,000).

Interest and other expense covers all the expenses that don't come from daily operations. If you have loans, as SOHO Equipment does, the interest you owe will show up here. *Profit before taxes* is just operating income minus interest and other expense. An example of "other expense" that would show up here is a loss (or gain) on the sale of a fixed asset such as a piece of machinery. Since that is a presumably a one-time transaction (accountants call it a *nonrecurring item*), it is handled separately on the income statement. SOHO Equipment's only entry in this category is $1,000 for the interest owed on its loan from Kyle Williams.

Income taxes is your accountant's estimate of what you owe the government on the profit you have made in the period covered by the income statement. Since SOHO Equipment made no profit in its first year, it doesn't have to set anything aside for taxes. (And since this isn't a book about taxes, we won't attempt to accurately calculate SOHO's tax liabilities in future years, either.)

Net profit (or *profit after tax*) is the famous "bottom line." It shows whether the company is making money on its sales, and how much. It's a measure of how much new wealth the company has created in a given period of time. This is a number that you really want to be positive and growing—although SOHO Equipment's negative number on this line, ($17,000), isn't so terrible, given that it's Bill and Carolyn's first year.

As noted above, many income statements use different terminology and show other items. They may break down the line items we've mentioned into smaller components. Check with your accountant about the finer details you may need on your own company's income statement. Then too, some companies focus on numbers that are derived from the income statement but aren't necessarily shown on it. For example, some track a measure known as *EBITDA*, which is an unwieldy acronym for "earnings before interest, taxes, depreciation, and amortization." EBITDA is typically figured by taking operating income and "adding back" depreciation and amortization. SOHO Equipment's EBITDA during the first year was ($5,000)—that is, ($16,000) in operating income plus $11,000 in depreciation and amortization. EBITDA is a popular measure among communications and entertainment companies, which must build complete networks and infrastructures before they begin to generate revenue. In their early years, therefore, net profit is nearly always negative. Focusing on EBITDA allows management to concentrate on current revenues and expenses.

No matter what your income statement looks like, always remember: *It has very little to do with cash actually going in and out the door.*

Sales, for example, are often called revenues. But the numbers don't show you how much cash flowed into your bank account. And COGS or COS shows you the costs of what you sold, as best as accountants can figure them. But those lines don't tell you what costs you actually wrote checks for during the time period in question.

Depreciation is just a number (accountants call it a *noncash charge*). Remember the florist who bought the truck for $25,000? The actual $25,000 purchase price may have been paid off long ago, or the florist may be paying it off in installments. But the depreciation expense will be determined by accounting rules for depreciating trucks, which are based on reasonable estimates of a truck's useful life, not by the amount of cash actually being laid out. It's the same with all the other items, right down to income tax expense. That "income taxes" line makes it look as if you're setting the money aside for the government, right? But nobody has actually taken any cash and put it into a separate bank account marked "taxes," and nobody has paid the government any money until the checks are actually mailed.

The fact is, the income statement is an *abstraction*. It's a useful abstraction because it answers that important question we posed at the beginning of this chapter. It shows you whether you're making money on the goods or services you provide, once you have taken all your costs and expenses into account. But it isn't real. It doesn't show how much cash you put in your bank account or how much cash you spent. In fact, if your company is growing fast, you may be building up inventory, buying new machinery, opening up new branches, and in general spending a whole lot more cash than you are generating. Your income statement may show that your company is highly profitable—and all the while you might be running out of cash!

There's another downside to accrual-based income statements. They provide a huge opportunity for what you might call creative accounting. Accountants are required to use a code of rules known as Generally Accepted Accounting Principles, or GAAP. The logic behind GAAP is reasonableness; the rules must make sense. Even so, there are many different rules within GAAP for treating depreciation, inventory, and so on. So to a limited extent accountants can choose how they calculate depreciation. They can select one or another method of valuing inventory. They can insert reserves for warranty costs, bad debt, and other eventualities—or not. They can record sales differently, depending on the likelihood of returns for credit. All such moves can be perfectly legal and perfectly consistent with accounting standards, but they will make the bottom line of the income statement look very different depending on which tactics the accountant chooses. (This is known as "the gap in GAAP.") Unless you're financially sophisticated, you can be fooled by clever accounting. And if you run your own business, what you really want to know isn't just the bottom line on an income statement, which is subject to all these accounting manipulations, but also how much cash is actually flowing into (and out of) your bank account.

This brings us to the next subject: cash flow.

FOUR

Cash Flow

The One Statement You *Really*
Can't Do Without

A POSITIVE BOTTOM LINE ON THE INCOME STATEMENT, showing that your company is making a profit, is surely a good thing. On the other hand, profitability is no guarantee of success or even survival. Every year, tens of thousands of businesses fail. Some were showing a profit at their demise. What happened? Simple: they didn't have enough cash to stay in business. They "grew broke."

"You can operate a long time without profit," said Lou Mobley, "but you can't survive one day without cash."

Cash is real money. It's what you have in the bank. Information about cash coming in and cash going out—*cash flow*—isn't abstract, it's concrete. A statement of cash flow doesn't reflect what things were worth five years ago, or how much they have depreciated since. It doesn't assume that you could sell everything in your inventory tomorrow. It tells you how much you deposited in your bank account, how much you wrote checks for, and what the difference was during a specific time span. Cash information helps lenders know whether you can pay them back. Cash information tells you whether you can buy a truck today and still make payroll next week.

Cash information is the other half of your business transactions, the part where you settle up accounts with your vendors and get paid by your customers. Just as the income statement has nothing to do with cash, the cash statement has nothing to do with promises and agreements, or accrual. It shows what's actually going in and going out. It tells you *how good a job you're doing at turning your profits into cash.*

Funny thing: before 1987, accountants had not done much to help companies track their cash—and we're looking all the way back to the fourteenth century.

The basics of accounting slowly began to evolve back then, as Venetian traders found they needed tools and techniques for keeping track of their expanding business ventures. And what reports did they come up with first? Balance sheets and income statements. Ever since, traditionally minded accountants have believed that the proper measures of a company's performance are profit, from the income statement, and solvency and liquidity, which can be calculated from the balance sheet. Cash was generally the focus of company treasurers, not of the accounting profession.

That began to change in 1987, when the Financial Accounting Standards Board (FASB, pronounced *faz-bee*) ruled that all financial statements involving CPAs must henceforth include a statement of cash flow. Unfortunately, FASB allowed accountants to prepare either direct or indirect cash-flow statements. Many chose (and still choose) indirect statements. Even though they're called cash-flow statements, they can include noncash items like depreciation. (We'll explain the difference in more detail below.) Even today, many accounting software packages don't let you compile a direct cash-flow statement. Some provide no cash-flow statement at all.

FASB's rule contained other sources of confusion as well. The board debated back and forth how various terms on the cash-flow statement would be defined and where they should appear. They decided, for example, that a line known as "net cash provided by operating activities"— one kind of bottom line on the cash-flow statement—would come after lines such as taxes and interest. In other words, as you worked your way down the cash-flow statement subtracting cash going out from cash coming in, you'd have to subtract taxes and interest payments before arriving at that "net" figure. Meanwhile, however, the line on the income statement labeled "operating income"—a line that plays much the same role on the income statement that "net cash from operating activities" plays on the cash-flow statement—is generally calculated *before* subtracting taxes and interest. So the two lines look similar but aren't even parallel in the way they're figured.

And then there's the question why accountants can't say something simple like "operating cash flow" instead of "net cash provided by operating activities"—but that's beyond the scope of this book!

Cash-flow statements are a great idea, but they haven't yet become well understood and well utilized, even by some accounting professionals. Maybe there hasn't been enough time. Maybe there hasn't been enough training. Your accountant might still tell you that you should rely on your income statement rather than your cash-flow statement to see how your company is doing—even though the whole point is to use *both*, not one or the other, along with the balance sheet.

Your accountant might also tell you that the indirect cash-flow statement he or she prepares is just fine. Trust us, it isn't. A *direct* cash-flow statement is analogous to a checkbook. It shows the cash that is actually coming in and going out, and it organizes these cash flows into categories that you'll find useful in managing the business. That's the kind of cash-flow statement we will describe in this chapter. The advantage of such a statement is that it clearly shows causes and effects and thus helps you understand how to correct any cash-flow problems you may have. An indirect cash-flow statement is different. To prepare one, an accountant begins with the income statement and makes various adjustments so that it shows cash flows. (An indirect cash-flow statement for SOHO Equipment, Inc. is presented in Appendix 1.) Even though an accurate indirect statement produces the same operating cash-flow figure as a direct one, the statement itself isn't intuitive, and so it's hard for non-financial people to understand and use.

If you do have to survive with an indirect cash-flow statement, it isn't the end of the world; only the presentation of operating cash flow is different. If it's at all possible, though, we suggest that you ask your accountant to compile a direct cash-flow statement showing what is going into and out of the bank. This kind of stand-alone statement meets the criteria for everything you'd want in a report about cash flow:

- It shows clearly whether the cash generated from everyday business operations (operating cash flow, or OCF) is positive or negative for the period of time you're looking at, and by how much.
- It shows how much cash was invested in the business, how much was received from lenders and investors, and how much was paid to lenders and investors.
- It shows whether the cash you received from all sources was more or less than the cash you paid out, and by how much.

Like the income statement, the cash-flow statement is a "movie" of events during a given time span. It shows you the other side, the cash side, of what happened in your business.

SOHO EQUIPMENT: FIRST-YEAR CASH FLOW

When we were reviewing Bill and Carolyn's start-up balance sheet, you may have noticed an important fact: they started SOHO Equipment with only $25,000 in cash. All the rest of the $215,000 they paid for Kyle Williams's assets went toward inventory, fixed assets, and goodwill. Twenty-five thousand dollars is a nice chunk of change, but it is not a lot of money for a business of this size to have in the bank. Every two weeks SOHO's payroll comes due and must be paid in cash. Every month, rent and office expenses have to be paid in cash. Granted, the company started out with $75,000 worth of inventory, which could be sold. But Bill and Carolyn not only had to sell it, they had to collect from their customers—and their new policy was to give customers thirty days to pay! Meanwhile, of course, Bill was ordering new inventory, and that would have to be paid for at some point in the not-too-distant future.

As it happened, cash was a constant headache during that first year. Bill and Carolyn didn't see the problem for a while because SOHO's customers still expected to pay on delivery, and a few of them actually did. (Bob Thomas, their first customer, wrote a check before Charlie had even finished installing the new system.) But as time went on, customers learned that they had thirty days to pay, and of course they took advantage of that fact. The company's cash situation grew more and more precarious. Payroll and other bills came due, relentlessly. Most of the vendors Bill dealt with were willing to extend SOHO credit on the basis of a personal guarantee from the new owners—but as soon as the payment term, ten days or thirty days or whatever, was up, they were on the phone wanting to know when they would be paid.

Bill had the job of managing the cash, and it took an inordinate amount of his time. He began offering customers discounts for early payments. He learned a dozen different ways of telling creditors "the check is in the mail" without actually using those words. He never actually missed a payroll, though he made one only by making the landlord wait an extra week for his rent check.

Finally, late in the fiscal year, Bill realized the truth: the company was running out of cash. It took him a while to come to this conclusion because he didn't entirely understand how it could be true. Sales were good. The accountant had told him that SOHO's operating loss would be small. Bill knew he was managing the cash as carefully as he could. So where was the problem? The fact was, he wasn't sure—but he could see that it wasn't going away. In late May, he visited the bank looking for a loan, only to learn that banks rarely lend money to small, struggling companies. In June, he persuaded Carolyn that they should take the only step open to them, applying for a home equity loan on top of their mortgage. They couldn't get much—only $11,000—but it was something, and it would tide them over. Once Bill and Carolyn had the money, they immediately turned around and loaned it to the company.

At the end of SOHO's first fiscal year, the company's accountant prepared a direct cash-flow statement. It looked like this:

TABLE 4.1   Cash-Flow Statement, SOHO Equipment, Year 1

Collections from customers	$470,000
Cash paid to suppliers (inventory paid)	(380,000)
Expenses paid (MSG&A paid)	(105,000)
Interest and other paid	(1,000)
Income taxes paid	(0)
Cash flow from operating activities (OCF)	(16,000)
Fixed asset investment	(0)
Other investments	0
Cash flow from investing activities (ICF)	0
Borrow (payback)	11,000
Paid in (paid out)	(0)
Dividends	0
Cash flow from financing activities (FCF)	11,000
Increase/decrease in cash (change in cash)	(5,000)
Beginning cash	25,000
Ending cash	$20,000

NOTE: How to read a cash-flow statement—We use a direct cash-flow statement in this book. This is a somewhat different format from the indirect cash-flow statements found in many companies' audited financial statements. Either cash-flow statement groups inflows and outflows of cash into three categories, depending on whether the transaction is related to operations, investing, or financing. (See the text for further explanation of these categories.)

In the statement above, the first five lines reflect cash transactions related to operations. Collections indicates cash coming in, while lines 2–5 reflect cash flowing out. These are subtotaled to yield cash flow from operating activities, or just operating cash flow (OCF). The second group of lines reflects transactions related to fixed assets and other investments (investing cash flow, or ICF), and the third group reflects transactions related to borrowing, stock sale, and other financing activities (financing cash flow, or FCF).

The three subtotals—OCF, ICF, and FCF—are then added to yield net change in cash, and this figure is added to beginning cash to yield ending cash. Parentheses in any line indicate a net outflow of cash, so the value is treated as a negative number when you're doing the subtotaling.

LINE ITEMS ON THE CASH-FLOW STATEMENT

Cash-flow statements aren't always identically formatted from one company to another. Still, most direct statements follow a pattern similar to SOHO's. Note that all the cash numbers are indicated as either positive or negative. (Positive numbers indicate an increase in cash; negative numbers indicate a decrease.) The reason is this: on a cash-flow statement, not all the inflows are at the top. Rather, the statement is divided into three categories, each with its related inflows and outflows.

Operating Cash Flow (OCF), or Cash Flow from Operating Activities

The first several lines on the statement reflect cash related to a business's operations. *Collections* is the top line and in ordinary circumstances represents a company's biggest inflow of cash. It's all the cash a business collects from outstanding receivables or from cash sales. Since this is cash flowing in, it's represented by a positive number. SOHO Equipment collected $470,000 from its customers during its first year.

Cash Paid to Suppliers or Inventory Paid.   This is cash that the business spent during the period to produce inventory. It includes cash spent on goods or materials that go into inventory and (in manufacturing companies) cash spent for the direct labor and factory overhead required to produce inventory. Remember the company that bought the golf shirts in March and sold them over the following three months? It would record a big inventory paid item in its cash-flow statement in whatever month it paid the bill for those shirts. SOHO Equipment spent $380,000 on goods for resale during the first year. Since this is cash flowing out, it counts as a negative number when you're adding up the line items. (In companies that do not have inventory, this item would probably be called costs paid.) Note that companies that buy inventory on credit can use the simple approach to cash-flow statements described in this chapter unless they are committed to tracking a measure called payable days. Payable days is discussed in Appendix 2.

Expenses Paid (MSG&A paid).   This includes all the checks a company writes to cover MSG&A expenses. Rent on the corporate office, the phone bill, office employees' paychecks—all that is included in this line item. Since SOHO (like other retailers) includes only the cost of goods for resale in its COGS and inventory paid lines, all other operating expenses are included under MSG&A and expenses paid. So the $105,000 spent during the first year includes payroll, rent, and so on. This item also counts as negative when you're adding up your cash flow.

Interest and Other Paid.   The $1,000 on SOHO's line is the interest paid to Kyle Williams on the note he holds. (No interest has yet been paid on Bill and Carolyn's own loan to the company; they'll probably put it off for a while, anyway.) This number is normally negative but it doesn't have to be. For example, if a company holds somebody else's debt and receives interest payments, that (positive) amount is included on this line. Payments for other expenses such as flood recovery would show up here as well.

Income Taxes Paid.   This item includes all the checks a company wrote to the federal and state governments for income taxes. This is always negative—unless for some reason you get a tax refund that's greater than your tax paid. SOHO's income tax payments, of course, are zero.

Although the cash-flow statement has three categories, it really has only one bottom line, OCF. *Cash flow from operating activities,* or *operating cash flow,* shows how much cash the company generated from operations. SOHO's is ($16,000), which helps you understand why that $25,000 that Bill and Carolyn started didn't give them much of a cushion.

Investing Cash Flow (ICF), or Cash Flow from Investing Activities

The second grouping of lines on the cash-flow statement reflects cash spent on investments, and the first item is *fixed asset investment.* This is the cash spent to buy plant, property, or equipment. Remember: it's cash, so there's no depreciation or any other abstraction involved. If you pay $25,000 cash for a delivery truck in August, your cash-flow statement for August shows a $25,000 item for fixed-asset investment. If your company spends cash on intangible assets such as a patent, on equity in another company, or on long-term certificates of deposit, that expenditure shows up on a second line, usually labeled *other investments*. SOHO Equipment spent nothing on fixed assets or other investments during the company's first year.

These lines are summed up as *cash flow from investing activities*, or *investing cash flow*. This number is usually negative because cash is flowing out. But in some circumstances it can be positive. For example, if you sell property, plant, or equipment—or if you receive cash from other investments—the amount received is recorded on this line and will offset any expenditure of cash.

Financing Cash Flow (FCF), or
Cash Flow from Financing Activities

The third grouping reflects cash received from or spent on financing activities. "Financing activities" is accountant-ese for money coming from (or going to) lenders and investors. It includes the following items.

Borrow (payback) is any cash received by the company from borrowing. If your business takes out a loan or draws on a line of credit, the cash is counted here. This line also includes any principal you paid back on a loan, so it can be a positive or negative number, depending on the difference between borrowing and payback in the time period covered by the cash-flow statement. (Remember that *interest* paid or received, however, shows up under operating cash flow.) The $11,000 loan SOHO received from its owners shows up here.

Paid in (paid out) is all cash received from stockholders for sale of stock, minus all cash paid to stockholders for stock buybacks. SOHO has nothing in either category during its first year of operation.

Dividends paid to stockholders are a separate line item. A cash withdrawal by a sole proprietor (usually called an *owner's draw*, not a dividend) may show up here. Again, SOHO has zero—from which we can conclude that Bill and Carolyn aren't taking any money out of the business yet. (Not surprising.)

Increase/decrease in cash or *change in cash* is the summation of the cash-flow statement. Change in cash is all the cash paid in to your company minus all the cash paid out. You arrive at this number simply by adding up all the others. Beginning cash shows what the company started with; ending cash is what it wound up with; change in cash is the difference. Unfortunately, SOHO ended up the year with $5,000 less in cash than it started with—even though it had received an $11,000 cash infusion from the loan.

DISSECTING THE CASH-FLOW STATEMENT

The real power of a stand-alone cash-flow statement lies in the fact that it can be broken down into these three categories, each of which reveals important information about a business. *Operating cash flow (OCF)* shows the cash a company is generating internally, from everyday business operations. *Investing cash flow (ICF)* covers cash spent for fixed assets and intangible assets, along with any receipts for the sale of fixed and intangible assets. *Financing cash flow (FCF)* shows cash received from lenders and investors minus any cash paid them. These three fit together in two simple equations:

$$OCF + ICF + FCF = change\ in\ cash$$

$$ending\ cash = beginning\ cash + change\ in\ cash$$

Knowing your operating, investing, and financing cash flows lets you manage your company's change in cash. If you have a recent cash-flow statement from your own company, you may want to get it out and analyze your own OCF, ICF, and FCF.

Operating Cash Flow

OCF is the lifeblood of a company. After all, a company generates cash in only three ways—from operations, from selling assets, and from lenders and investors (borrowing money or selling stock). But cash from operations is the most important of the three. No company can live long on the basis of selling assets. And if you can't generate cash from operations, lenders and investors aren't usually going to be willing to give you their money. So a healthy OCF is one big key to a successful business. You should be thinking about your OCF every day and checking it every month. This is the most important line on the cash-flow statement, more important than ending cash or change in cash or anything else. You can be GE or Microsoft, but if you don't have a healthy ongoing OCF you're on the way down. The companies that really need a lot of cash in the bank are those that *don't* have a healthy OCF, those that are just starting up and don't expect to have positive OCF for a while, or those that don't have a financing line in place.

Investing Cash Flow

When you analyze ICF, the most important line to look at is the amount spent on fixed assets. This is a good measure of your company's investment in its future. If you're hoping to get outside investment some day, for example, investors will look carefully at your level of fixed-asset investment and at the trend in fixed-asset investment over time. What's more, if you compare OCF to fixed-asset investment, you can see whether you are funding your fixed-asset investment without having to borrow or sell more stock. Single out OCF and ICF on the cash-flow statement, compare them, and you'll get a very good indication of how your company is financing its fixed-asset investment. Some capital-intensive, high-growth companies will maintain an ICF greater than OCF for a period of years. Over the long term, however, most companies want OCF to be greater than ICF—that is, they want to fund investment internally so as to reduce their dependence on outside sources of financing.

Financing Cash Flow

FCF, finally, shows your relationship to (and dependence on) investors and lenders. Are you repaying your outstanding loans or is your

indebtedness growing? Are you having to sell more stock in your company to finance your cash needs? Are you paying your shareholders dividends? Total FCF can be positive or negative, depending on a business's
circumstances. But the owner of the business must always know why it
is what it is—in other words, where the cash is going and where it's
coming from.

Before we leave the subject of cash, we want to tell a story about a company you'd think would hardly have to worry about cash flow, General
Electric. Jack Welch took over GE as CEO around 1980 and proceeded
to transform it. He reduced the payroll substantially. He sold off dozens
of businesses and acquired dozens of others. Not everybody likes to give
"Neutron Jack" credit, but there's no denying that his moves paid off
handsomely in terms of profitability. GE's net profits have increased
about 10 percent per year since Welch took over.

Given the way the stock market values companies, you would expect
GE's stock price to rise about 10 percent per year as well. And so it did,
until the early 1990s. Then the stock price failed to keep up with earnings growth. Welch consulted with his financial experts to figure out
why. One of them pointed out that, although net profit was increasing
10 percent per year, cash flow wasn't growing nearly as fast. Perhaps
some astute investors were questioning the quality of GE's earnings. After all, GE didn't seem to be doing that great a job at turning its profits
into cash.

In late 1991, Welch decided to refocus his managers' attention on
cash flow as well as on profitability. Communications from the executive offices emphasized the importance of cash flow. Everyone in top
management talked about it. In some cases, incentive compensation
was changed to reward improvements in asset management. Pretty soon
managers began getting the message. And once they did, they began
taking action. They found new ways to warehouse inventory to get
products to customers faster. They began using electronic data inter-
change (EDI) to bill customers and collect from them. They began
negotiating more favorable payment terms with both customers and
suppliers.

A little more than a year later, GE's 1992 annual report showed that the company's net profit was again up by about 10 percent. OCF, however, increased from $7.5 billion to $10 billion, or 33 percent. And sure enough, over a parallel twelve-month period, GE's stock price rose from $74 per share to $96 per share, or 30 percent. (These amounts are in 1992 dollars and are unadjusted for subsequent events such as stock splits). The moral: both profit and cash flow are important, no matter how big you are—and no matter how small you are.

This chapter completes the review of the three key financial statements. But knowing what's on each statement is really only the beginning of *using* your financials to run a better business. Next, it's important to understand how the statements fit together. That will enable you to see the big financial picture of what's going on in your company.

PART TWO

Understanding the Big Picture

FIVE

The Three Bottom Lines

And What They Tell You

HAVE YOU EVER WATCHED PEOPLE WHO REALLY KNOW WHAT they're doing pore over a set of financial statements? We're thinking of savvy investors, smart lenders, sophisticated business owners, and financial executives. They spread the papers out in front of them. They go back and forth from the income statement to the balance sheet to the cash-flow statement. (If there isn't a cash-flow statement, you can be sure they'll request one.) They ask for more information—last year's data, the year before that, even the year before that—and they start making trend charts. Pretty soon they begin asking all kinds of questions. And if you know anything about the company they're examining, you realize the truth: these people learn a phenomenal amount about a business just by studying the numbers. They can spot its strengths. They understand some of its vulnerabilities and challenges. They often know enough to decide whether it's worth investing in or lending money to.

Think how valuable it would be if you could do this for your own business. Think how valuable it would be if you really understood the whole story—the financial big picture—every time you received a set of financial statements.

The value is almost incalculable. Because if you can understand what they tell you, a complete set of financials is like a set of powerful lenses.

Some of the lenses are wide-angle, showing you what your company's overall results are. Others give you close-up views; they help you understand nitty-gritty details such as the reason your receivables have been on the rise. With this information, you can manage your business intelligently, so as to optimize its performance and achieve your goals. Without the information, you're flying blind. You don't really know how your company is performing and you don't really know why its performance might be improving or declining.

The first step in understanding and using the financials in this way is to familiarize yourself with the tools of the trade. That means knowing what a balance sheet, an income statement, and a cash-flow statement are, and what kinds of information they contain. If you're still not sure what *equity* is or how *profit* differs from *cash*, please go back and review Part 1 of this book. Learning the financials is like learning any skill. There's no avoiding the basics.

Now comes the fun part: understanding what these three statements tell you, why you need all three, and how they fit together.

Maybe you studied a foreign language in school. Do you remember that wonderful eureka moment when you realized, *Hey, I understand this stuff!* All of a sudden it wasn't just strange-sounding words and boring rules, it was a language with meaning, and you could see and hear things that you couldn't see or hear before. That's what we hope to do for financial statements in this section of the book: show you the meaning of all those terms and numbers and how they fit together. Then, in Part 3, we'll show you how to put your knowledge to work in running your company.

We'll begin with the fact that a well-run business has three important financial statements and that each financial statement has its own important bottom line.

THREE BOTTOM LINES

The idea that a company has three bottom lines catches a lot of businesspeople by surprise. After all, everyone knows that the financial goal of a business is to make a profit—to increase this *one* bottom line.

If only it were so simple! If it were, we wouldn't need anything more than an income statement to see how a company was performing. But the world is rarely as simple as we'd like it to be. If you have been around the business world for a while, you know that profit alone is never a sufficient measure of a company's performance. Companies can be profitable but go belly-up. Companies can be increasing their profits while actually performing worse than before. Companies can be making a profit that looks like a lot of money in dollar terms. But if you stop and analyze the profit, you realize the shareholders would be better off investing in CDs or Treasury bills.

How can this be? The answer is that *profit is only one measure of a business's financial performance*. It isn't a bad measure, but it can't do the measurement job by itself. As noted in Part 1, you can't get an accurate picture of a company's financials without three separate statements. And you can't judge a company's performance with fewer than three distinct bottom lines. Not surprisingly, each bottom line derives primarily from one of the financial statements. And like the financial statements themselves, each has distinct advantages and disadvantages.

Net profit is the first of the three bottom lines. It comes from the income statement (Table 3.1), and it shows whether your company's sales in any given time span exceeds its costs. It shows whether you're "making money."

As a performance measurement, net profit has a lot to recommend it. The business world understands it. It can't be distorted by unpredictable variations in a company's cash flow. It spreads depreciation over an asset's useful life, so that, for example, your profit doesn't disappear just because you bought an expensive new machine.

But net profit also has many drawbacks as a measurement. If you keep an eye only on net profit, for example, you may be able to keep expenses from exceeding sales. But you won't know how much cash is actually going into your bank account. Maybe your receivables are increasing. Maybe you are spending more than you need to spend on inventory. If all your profits are tied up in receivables and inventory, you may run out of cash and have to suspend operations even though you are ostensibly making money. Short of that, you may be doing a poor job at managing your cash and managing your fixed assets. You might be turning a profit, but is it really more than you could earn if you liquidated the business, took the money, and invested in T-bills? How do you know?

Another drawback of profit as a metric: it is susceptible to accounting distortions. When accountants figure net profit, they often can choose among various legitimate methods of calculating depreciation and valuing inventories. Profit will vary depending on which method they choose. Remember the point made in Part 1: the income statement is an abstraction. So profit is an abstraction too.

Operating cash flow (OCF) is a great second bottom line. You find it on the cash-flow statement (Table 4.1). It shows how much net cash is flowing into your company, independent of what you may receive from lenders and investors and independent of what you spend on fixed assets or other investments. It shows the cash you're generating from operations.

Why is it helpful? Unlike net profit, OCF is based on real events—cash going in and cash going out—and not on accounting theory. Because of this, OCF can't be manipulated internally, merely by following different rules for preparing the financials. If your OCF is consistently positive, you know you are generating enough cash from operations to meet your regular obligations.

OCF can also be used to test the quality of a company's earnings (or profit). Are the profits on the income statement real or have they somehow been manipulated? This was what investors may have been worrying about when GE's stock price didn't rise as fast as its profits. There are plenty of other examples of this concern. Around 1994, for example, Kodak changed its depreciation method, which made its profits look larger than they otherwise would have. However, investors who checked the company's operating cash flow (and the footnotes to its financial statements) could see that Kodak's financial performance wasn't as good as it first appeared from the income statement.

In general, OCF should consistently be larger than net profit. If it is, that's a sign that a business is doing a good job of managing assets such as receivables and inventory. Financial people say that it is doing a good job of *turning its profits into cash*. If OCF is consistently smaller than net profit, the company is doing a poor job. In some cases, fraud has been discovered when OCF was consistently lower than net profit.

So why not use OCF as a single bottom line? Unfortunately, it too can be manipulated—not internally, by choosing different accounting procedures, but externally. For instance, a company can arrange or decide to pay its vendors late, temporarily increasing OCF. It can also increase OCF by sacrificing profitability, which is not necessarily wise. In some industries, for example, it is common for an operating company to sell its accounts receivable to another business known as a factor. The factor pays so much on the dollar for the receivables and then attempts to collect the full amount, which is how it makes money. The operating company trades $1.00 worth of receivables for (say) $.85 worth of cash. This move obviously improves the company's immediate operating cash flow. But it can hurt immediate profits because a sale worth $1.00 has effectively been transformed into a sale worth $.85.

Return on assets (ROA) is the third bottom line. It's calculated by taking net profit (from the income statement) and dividing by average assets. Assets are found on the balance sheet (Table 2.3). To find average assets for a given time period, you just add the assets at the beginning and the assets at the end, then divide by two. For example, if a company has $1 million in assets at the beginning of a year and $1.2 million at the end, its average assets for the year are $1.1 million. If it made $100,000 in net profit during the year, its ROA is $100,000 divided by $1,100,000, or approximately 9 percent.

ROA is a terrific bottom line. It encompasses net profit, so it shows you whether you're doing a good job managing sales and expenses. It also shows you how effectively you're managing assets such as receivables, inventory, and fixed assets. ROA helps you evaluate what's really happening when your profit moves in one direction or the other. If your profit has risen but ROA has declined, for instance, it means your assets have grown faster than your profits. That's usually a sign that you're not managing your assets effectively.

ROA has one other big advantage: it allows a company to compare itself to competitors in the same industry. Profit levels and cash flow can differ widely from one company to another. But ROA is a kind of universal solvent for companies in the same business: it shows how much profit a company is earning for a given level of total assets.

Why not just use ROA? One reason is that it's a little more complex than the other measures and so can be harder for people without financial training to understand. But the real reason is that it too is an abstraction. The numerator (net profit) has the drawbacks we described above. The denominator (average assets) depends on how accountants value inventory, how they depreciate fixed assets, and so on. ROA is a good measure; it just isn't perfect—and it still doesn't tell you how much cash you netted last month!

The truth is, you need all three bottom lines. You need all three measures. Without them, you just can't see the big picture. Your company can look good in terms of dollar profits but poor when you consider ROA. Your company can be earning a profit but be unable to meet payroll because there's not enough cash. Your company can have a satisfactory ROA but flat or declining sales—a possible recipe for disaster. With all three, however, you can tell if you're really making money. Just like the experts at the beginning of this chapter, you can "read the tea leaves" and identify your business's strengths and weaknesses. More important, you can use the knowledge you gain to manage the business more effectively. From a financial perspective, improvement on the three bottom lines is the goal of a business.

In a few industries, companies find that the three bottom lines as we have defined them are not the most useful tools for evaluating performance. One company we are familiar with in the cellular telephone business focuses on EBITDA—earnings before interest, taxes, depreciation, and amortization—as a measure of profitability, and on a measure they call free cash flow, which is operating cash flow minus capital expenditures, as a measure of cash flow. In the cable television industry, many firms track EBITDA and also EBITDA minus capital expenditures, which is what *they* call free cash flow.

Whatever the variations, however, every company needs to make a profit, generate cash, and produce sufficient return on investment to be competitive. These three bottom lines, which we define here generically, give you a powerful tool for evaluating a business's performance. And the great thing is, you don't need a degree in finance to understand and use them. All you need is a little practice.

TREND ANALYSIS

Here's one more point to keep in mind when you're assessing financial performance. Remember how we noted that financial experts always seem to want more years' worth of data? And how they're likely to start building trend charts? The reason is simple: a company's financials for one time period, however complete, are a fine starting point, but they don't tell you much by themselves. What you really want to know about a business is how it performs *over time*, and whether its performance on those three bottom lines is improving or declining.

You'd think this would be obvious. But it happens over and over: business owners are asked for a set of financials, maybe by a prospective lender. They come back with one balance sheet, one income statement, and perhaps one cash-flow statement. From the lender's perspective, this is like the Boston Red Sox fan who returned after four years on a desert island and asked how the Red Sox had been doing. The answer he got—"they whipped the Yankees yesterday"—was cheery. But it told him nothing about the season as a whole, let alone how they had done during the preceding four years.

For one year, a complete set of financials includes *two* balance sheets—beginning and ending—and an income statement and a cash-flow statement. That at least lets you see how the balance sheet changed over the year. But to evaluate a business effectively, you typically need at least three years' worth of financials, showing all three bottom lines. That lets you chart net profit, operating cash flow, and return on assets over time. It shows you where the real strengths and weaknesses lie. Just as a baseball coach would analyze offensive statistics, pitching statistics, and defensive statistics, you can analyze every aspect of your company's financial performance over time. If the statements are set up in columns to allow easy year-to-year comparison, so much the better. Ideally, your financial statements should let you see at a glance whether and where you're winning or losing—and not just yesterday but over a meaningful time span.

In Part 3, we'll analyze the performance of SOHO Equipment over just such a three-year period. First, however, it's important to see how the three statements fit together—and how you can capture the big financial picture of a company all on one page.

SIX

The Financial Scoreboard

Seeing the Big Picture—At a Glance

ALL THREE OF THE KEY FINANCIAL STATEMENTS FIT TO-gether like a jigsaw puzzle. Changes in one statement have effects on the others. If you know the connections, you can show exactly how each of those changes is related. You can also put all the statements side by side and see those connections at a glance. We call this the "big picture."

How the financials fit together isn't magic; in fact it's really quite simple. Still, no one seems to have done it effectively until IBM executive Lou Mobley came along. Despite his very successful career—which included being founding director of IBM's famous Executive School—Lou realized that he really didn't understand financial statements. He also realized that many of the students at the Executive School didn't understand them either. The financial managers seemed to speak one language. The nonfinancial folks seemed to speak another. When they got into debates, the financial folks usually seemed to win because their opponents didn't know how to answer their jargon-filled arguments. Mobley wanted everybody to speak the same language so they could work together better.

So Mobley began teaching himself to understand financials. What he found—surprise!—was that most of his assumptions about financial statements weren't true. He had thought a company's income statement had something to do with the cash it took in and the cash it laid out. He thought "cost of goods sold" must be what a company spent to acquire inventory in a given period. As he studied the basics, he once wrote, "one myth after another had to be washed from my mind."

But he learned those basics—the very same material we have presented in the previous chapters of this book. Then he began asking how the various financial statements fit together.

The trouble with conventional financial statements isn't just that they're fragmented; it's also that the connections between them aren't apparent. Looking at this year's balance sheet compared to last year's doesn't tell you *why* you have more cash (say) now than you did then or why your liabilities rose even faster than your cash. You might look to your income statement or your cash-flow statement (if you have one) to explain the differences, but you won't find it easy going. These statements just aren't set up to answer these cause-and-effect questions.

Once you do understand the cause-and-effect connections, however, you begin to see the big picture. That's what Mobley realized—and that's what we want to show you.

To begin, let's imagine that Bill and Carolyn Michaels want to assess the performance of their company, SOHO Equipment, during its first year of operation. Their starting point, naturally, is the balance sheet at the start of the year, when they first bought the company. (The balance sheet, remember, is a snapshot of the company's financial condition at a particular point in time.) That balance sheet looked like Table 6.1.

Their ending point, similarly, would be the balance sheet at the end of the first year (See Table 6.2 on page 64.).

Right away you'll notice that quite a lot changed in this company's financial situation. The amount of cash in the bank decreased by $5,000. Accounts receivable went up, from zero at inception to $30,000. Inventory rose by $30,000. Gross fixed assets stayed the same, while net fixed assets—thanks to a year's worth of depreciation—declined. Goodwill also declined, from $15,000 to $14,000. On the liabilities side, accounts payable went from zero to $50,000, while long-term debt rose from $10,000 to $21,000, reflecting the $11,000 loan to the company from its owners. Retained earnings is a negative number, so the Michaels'

TABLE 6.1　Balance Sheet, SOHO Equipment,
Start-Up

Assets	
Cash and cash equivalents	$ 25,000
Accounts receivable	0
Inventory	75,000
Notes receivable	0
Current assets	100,000
Gross fixed assets	100,000
Less accumulated depreciation	(0)
Net fixed assets	100,000
Goodwill, net	15,000
Other investments	0
Total assets	$215,000
Liabilities and equity	
Accounts payable	$　　0
Taxes payable	0
Other liabilities	0
Current liabilities	0
Long-term debt	10,000
Total liabilities	10,000
Common stock	205,000
Retained earnings	0
Total equity	205,000
Total liabilities & equity	$215,000

equity in the company actually declined. (Remember that fundamental equation: assets equals liabilities plus equity.)

So what actually happened *during* the year to produce all these changes? If you're like a lot of business owners, you turn next to the income statement for 1998. SOHO Equipment's is shown in Table 6.3.

Some of the numbers on the income statement do seem to explain the changes on the balance sheet. Check that net profit number, for example, of ($17,000). That's the same as the retained earnings on the balance sheet. And depreciation on the income statement is the same as accumulated depreciation on the balance sheet. (Of course, that's the case

TABLE 6.2   Balance Sheet, SOHO Equipment, End Year 1

Assets	
Cash and cash equivalents	$ 20,000
Accounts receivable	30,000
Inventory	105,000
Notes receivable	0
Current assets	155,000
Gross fixed assets	100,000
Less accumulated depreciation	(10,000)
Net fixed assets	90,000
Goodwill, net	14,000
Other investments	0
Total assets	$259,000
Liabilities and equity	
Accounts payable	$ 50,000
Taxes payable	0
Other liabilities	0
Current liabilities	50,000
Long-term debt	21,000
Total liabilities	71,000
Common stock	205,000
Retained earnings	(17,000)
Total equity	188,000
Total liabilities & equity	$259,000

because we're looking at only one year's worth of accumulated depreciation; after the first year, the two numbers won't match.)

The other numbers, however, don't seem to explain much. The income statement contains no cash information, so it isn't going to explain how Bill and Carolyn wound up with less cash at the end of the year than they started with. Nor can they tell from the income statement why receivables and inventory increased. Where are the numbers that will answer these questions?

If your answer is "on the cash-flow statement," you're right. So let's examine SOHO's cash-flow statement for Year 1 (Table 6.4).

TABLE 6.3 Income Statement, SOHO Equipment, Year 1

Sales	$500,000
Cost of goods sold	350,000
Gross profit	150,000
Depreciation	10,000
Goodwill amortization	1,000
Marketing & selling expense	25,000
General & administrative expense	130,000
Operating income	(16,000)
Interest and other expenses	1,000
Profit before taxes	(17,000)
Income taxes	0
Net profit	$(17,000)

TABLE 6.4 Cash-Flow Statement, SOHO Equipment, Year 1

Collections from customers	$470,000
Cash paid to suppliers (inventory paid)	(380,000)
Expenses paid (MSG&A paid)	(105,000)
Interest and other paid	(1,000)
Income taxes paid	(0)
Cash flow from operating activities (OCF)	(16,000)
Fixed asset investment	(0)
Other investments	(0)
Cash flow from investing activities (ICF)	(0)
Borrow (payback)	11,000
Paid in (paid out)	0
Dividends	(0)
Cash flow from financing activities (FCF)	11,000
Increase/decrease in cash (change in cash)	(5,000)
Beginning cash	25,000
Ending cash	$20,000

One number leaps out: ($5,000) for "increase/decrease in cash." That's exactly the difference in the cash line (the top line) between the start-up balance sheet and the year-end balance sheet.

Now consider another change between the two balance sheets, namely, the increase in accounts receivable from zero to $30,000 during the year. First, think for a moment about what affects receivables. One factor is obviously sales—and sales of $500,000 are recorded on the income statement. But Bill and Carolyn also need to know how much of those sales they actually collected. That number is over on the cash statement: $470,000 in "collections."

So calculating the change in receivables is a simple matter of arithmetic. Take SOHO's start-up receivables of zero. *Add* the $500,000 in sales (since this amount constitutes new receivables) and *subtract* the $470,000 in collections (this amount is no longer "receivable," since it has been paid). Presto: year-end receivables of $30,000!

Now let's figure out why inventory increased by $30,000. Remember two things. First, cost of goods sold (COGS), which appears on the income statement, is a measure of "inventory out"—in other words, the number of units sold times the cost of each unit. Second, cash paid to suppliers—inventory paid, on the cash-flow statement—shows how much a company actually spent to increase its inventory. The net of those two numbers explains the difference in year-end inventory. Beginning inventory of $75,000 minus COGS of $350,000 (inventory out— that's why it's minus) plus inventory paid of $380,000 equals ending inventory of $105,000. In other words, $30,000 more inventory came in than went out.

The fact is, *you can account for almost every single change that occurs from one balance sheet to the next by taking the appropriate numbers from the income statement and the cash statement and adding or subtracting them.*

Mobley wasn't alone in discovering this relationship. If you dig deep enough into the work papers of a corporate auditor, you'll find individual line items reconciled in much the same way that we just did. But accountants in general don't talk much about how all the numbers fit together. They rarely explain the connections to business owners, and they haven't learned to present financial statements in such a way that the connections are clear. As we mentioned, many accountants don't even produce a direct cash-flow statement—which leaves owners and managers trying to puzzle out exactly what produced the changes from one balance sheet to the next.

Once Mobley understood the connections, he invented a name for them, the *continuity equation*. Then he created a simple one-page matrix showing the beginning balance sheet, the income statement, the cash-flow statement, and the ending balance sheet. His students promptly dubbed it the Mobley Matrix. We have rechristened it the Financial Scoreboard.

The basic idea of the Financial Scoreboard is simplicity itself. Put the beginning balance sheet on the left-hand side of the page. Put the income statement next to it, and the cash-flow statement next to that, and the ending balance sheet on the right-hand side of the page. But there are two secrets to making it work.

First, you have to do some rearranging from the conventional formats, so that the right numbers line up horizontally. For example, "change in cash" must be at the top of the cash-flow statement so that it aligns with the "cash" line on the balance sheets.

Second, the signs of the numbers will be different, depending on whether you're adding them up vertically or horizontally. For instance, look at the "collections" number in the cash-flow statement. When you're adding up the cash-flow statement itself—we call this "doing the vertical math"—collections is obviously a positive number, since it represents cash coming in. When you're figuring out the ending balance sheet, however—"doing the horizontal math"—you're adding sales to beginning receivables and *subtracting* collections to get ending receivables. So here collections is treated as a negative number.

It's easy to get confused by this at first. However, the different signs reflect common-sense logic. For example, look at the figure for income tax paid on the cash statement. That's a minus in vertical math because it reduces cash—it's a cash outflow. It's also a minus on horizontal math because it reduces income tax due on the ending balance sheet. By contrast, look at fixed asset investment on the cash statement. That's also a

TABLE 6.5 Financial Scoreboard,[a] SOHO Equipment, Year 1 ($000)

Days: 365

Beginning Balance Sheet 12/31/00		Income Statement		Cash Statement		Ending Balance Sheet 12/31/01	
Cash	25	Sales	500	Cash Change	−5	Cash	20
Accounts Receivable	0	Cost of Goods Sold	350	Collections (OCF)	470	Accounts Receivable	30
Inventory	75			Inventory Paid (OCF)	380	Inventory	105
Other Operating Assets	0			Prepayments (OCF)	0	Other Operating Assets	0
Notes Receivable–Trade	0			Lend (Receive) (OCF)	0	Notes Receivable–Trade	0
Gross Fixed Assets	100	Depreciation+Amortization	10	Fixed Asset Investment (ICF)	0	Gross Fixed Assets	100
Accumulated Depreciation	0	Intangible Amortization	1			Accumulated Depreciation	10
Net Fixed Assets	100					Net Fixed Assets	90
Other Investments	15			Other Investment (ICF)	0	Other Investments	14
Total Assets	215					Total Assets	259
Accounts Payable	0	MSG&A Expense	155	Expense Paid (OCF)	105	Accounts Payable	50
Debt	10			Borrow (Payback) (FCF)	11	Debt	21
Other Operating Liabilities	0	Interest & Other Expenses	1	Interest & Other Paid (OCF)	1	Other Operating Liabilities	0
Income Tax Due	0	Income Tax Expense	0	Income Tax Paid (OCF)	0	Income Tax Due	0
Nonoperating Liabilities	0	Nonoperating Expense	0	NonoperatingExpPaid(FCF)	0	Nonoperating Liabilities	0
Stock	205			Paid In (FCF)	0	Stock	205
Retained Earnings	0	>>>Net Profit	−17	Dividend & Other (FCF)	−17	Retained Earnings	−17
Total Liabilities + Equity	215	>>>Return on Assets	−7.17%	>>>Operating Cash Flow	−16	Total Liabilities + Equity	259

[a] Financial Scoreboard/Mobley Matrix™ ©Compilation Copyright

TABLE 6.6   Financial Scoreboard
Decoder (income statement) — "Vertical
Math"

+	Sales
–	Cost of goods sold
–	Depreciation/amortization
–	Intangible amortization
–	MSG&A expense
–(+)	Interest and other expense (inc.)
–	Income tax expense
=	Net profit

minus in vertical math because it represents a cash outflow. But it's a plus in horizontal math because cash spent on fixed assets obviously increases gross fixed assets on the ending balance sheet. The logic here is that *the financial statements show cause-and-effect relationships, and the causes have different effects depending on where they show up on the financials.*

TABLE 6.7   Financial Scoreboard
Decoder (cash-flow statement) —
"Vertical Math"

=	Change in cash
+	Collections (OCF)[a]
–	Inventory paid (OCF)[a]
–	Prepayment (OCF)[a]
–	Fixed asset investment (ICF)[b]
–	Other investment (ICF)[b]
–	Expense paid (OCF)[a]
+(–)	Borrow (payback) (FCF)[c]
–	Interest and other paid (OCF)[a]
–	Income tax paid (OCF)[a]
+	Paid in (FCF)[c]
–	Dividends and other (FCF)[c]

[a] Operating cash flow
[b] Investing cash flow
[c] Financing cash flow

To help you check your logic on any given item, we have developed a decoder for the Financial Scoreboard. The decoder shows whether you add or subtract depending on whether you're doing "vertical math" or "horizontal math." For example, start with a generic income statement. Run the numbers downward. You start with sales, subtract all the various costs and expenses, and wind up with net profit. Every line except sales is treated as negative.

For the cash statement on the Scoreboard, use the cash-flow decoder. Start at the bottom and run the numbers *upward*. You wind up with change in cash, the figure at the top.

Finally, let's look in detail at the horizontal math. Some of the signs are different than they are in vertical math because we're looking at the effect of changes on individual line items. Take payables, for example. Payables are *increased* by whatever expenses a company incurs on the MSG&A line of the income statement. Payables are *decreased* by the expense paid line on the cash-flow statement. Start with beginning payables, add MSG&A expense, subtract expense paid, and you wind up with ending payables.

What good does it do to put all these numbers together on one page? After all, the Scoreboard isn't a replacement for the three traditional financial statements; it's just another way of arranging them. But the Financial Scoreboard has several big advantages over the traditional presentation.

- It lets you see the big picture of your company's financials at a glance. It's like an executive summary.
- It shows cause-and-effect relationships. You can understand exactly how and why your balance sheet at the end of a year (or a month) differs from the balance sheet of the preceding period. You can see why receivables went up or down, why inventory has increased or decreased, and where the change on the cash line came from. The Scoreboard thus makes it easy to track progress against goals.
- It helps you fill in gaps. If you don't get a direct cash-flow statement from your accountant, for example, you can create one using the Scoreboard.

TABLE 6.8 Financial Scoreboard Decoder—"Horizontal Math"

Balance Sheet (start)	Income Statement	Cash-Flow Statement	Balance Sheet (end)
+ Cash		+ Change in cash	= Cash
+ Receivables	+ Sales	– Collections	= Receivables
+ Inventory	– Cost of goods sold	+ Inventory paid	= Inventory
+ Other operating assets		+ Prepayment	= Other operating assets
+ Gross fixed assets		+ Fixed asset investment	= Gross fixed assets
+ Accum. depreciation	+ Depreciation/amortization		= Accum. depreciation
+ Other investment	– Intangible amortization	+ Other investment	= Other investment
+ Payables	+ MSG&A expense	– Expense paid	= Payables
+ Debt		+(–) Borrow (payback)	= Debt
+ Other operating liabilities	+(–) Interest & other exp. (inc.)	– Interest & other paid	= Other operating liabilities
+ Income taxes due	+ Income tax expense	– Income tax paid	= Income taxes due
+ Stock		+ Paid in	= Stock
+ Retained earnings	+ Net profit	– Dividends & other	= Retained earnings

- It's a powerful planning tool, as we'll see in Chapter 12. You can plug in projected figures for the *coming* period of time, then watch what happens to some of the other items on the Scoreboard.
- It's helpful in detecting error, incompetence, and even fraud. If things don't add up, you know there are mistakes in the traditional financials.

The Scoreboard works for any company, anywhere: big, small, manufacturer, service, retail, whatever. Entrepreneurs use it. So do divisions of big companies. Pentax used it to help its managers understand their Japanese parent company's statements. GE Europe used it to train salespeople from thirteen countries, most of whom spoke different languages. It's only a matter of time before most businesses realize just how powerful a tool it is.

At this point, you should have a better understanding of your financial statements—and more confidence in your ability to interpret them. But understanding and interpretation are only the first steps. The next step is learning to use your financial statements to manage your business. In the following section we'll look at the key numbers and ratios you can pull off your financials. Then we'll show you how to use the Financial Scoreboard not just to understand your company's financial performance but to manage it—to set goals and reach them.

PART THREE

Financial Analysis to Boost Performance

SEVEN

The Three Financial Goals

And Some Perspective on Them

S O WHAT'S THE POINT OF ALL THIS FINANCIAL ANALYSIS, anyway? It isn't to make work for the accountants (though it does). And it isn't to have something impressive to show your banker (though it may help on that score). The point is to help you manage your business more effectively and to reach your financial goals.

Before you put all this data to use, however, it's wise to put things in perspective. For example, notice that word *goals*. We assume that you want to have a successful, moneymaking business. Beyond that, we don't have any idea what your goals might be. Maybe you want to be the next Bill Gates. Perhaps you want to run a small family company that you can pass along to your children. Maybe you hope to build up the business over five years, then sell it and play golf. Any of these goals (and many others) are worthwhile objectives. The important thing is that you *know what your goals are*. Financial analysis can show you how you're doing on the road to your goals. But *you* have to determine the destination; otherwise you won't know what the numbers are telling you.

Most financial advisers generally like to see companies with strong balance sheets—not too much debt compared to equity—and healthy net profit. But if you're in a start-up situation, for example, your balance sheet may look weak and your profit may be small or even negative. Is this so bad? Not necessarily, as long as you're clear on your goals and you have a plan for reaching them. Eventually you will need to earn a profit, achieve positive operating cash flow (OCF), and record a healthy return on assets (ROA). Your plan should specify when you expect to reach each milestone and what you're going to do in the meantime. If it will be a while before you achieve a positive OCF, for example, you need a reliable source of financing cash flow to cover whatever deficits you may be running up. And you need to watch your change in cash on the cash-flow statement to be sure you're not consuming your cash faster than you had planned on.

Another word of perspective: not everything that's important about a business is captured in the financials. To be successful in running a company, you need to do a lot of things right. You need to offer a product or service at a price customers are willing to pay. You need to mount effective sales and marketing campaigns. You need to hire good people and lead them well. You need to make plans for the long term as well as the short term, and to figure out the appropriate balance between them. Financials can tell you how you're doing at managing *the parts of your business that can be measured in dollars.* That's a lot—but it's not everything. The financials you get today can't tell you how loyal your customers will be tomorrow. They can't tell you that a competitor is about to come out with a new product that's better than yours. They can't tell you where to find—and how to select—the best people.

Finance is extremely important. If you want to run a successful company, you need the kind of insight into your performance that only a good set of financials can provide. But you must know where you want to go, and you must pay equal attention to all the nonfinancial aspects of running a company.

From a financial perspective, the job of a company owner (or any business manager) is relatively simple. That job is to manage *sales, expenses,* and *assets* in such a way that the company reaches its financial goals. These are the three key numbers, and they're often captured in the acronym SEA. Nonfinancial goals may differ from one company to another, but the three financial goals are essentially the same for all businesses:

- Most companies must make a profit in the short term, and all companies must make a profit in the long term. And not just any amount of profit: they must make *enough* profit to reinvest for the future, to pay dividends to shareholders, or both. For the typical company, of course, the long term isn't any different from the short term: it needs to make money right now. We stuck the qualification in there to remind you that start-up and fast-growth companies often don't make money right away, and that even well-established companies can afford an occasional year in which they sacrifice profit in pursuit of some other goal (such as expansion).

- Companies must generate sufficient cash to pay their bills. This is an immediate concern. (Remember Mobley's dictum: you can operate for a long time without profit, but you can't operate one day without cash.) Again, some young high-growth companies don't expect operating cash flow to be positive for some time. Many of these are high-tech operations with substantial venture-capital backing. But these companies must monitor the rate at which they're consuming their cash, and they need a plan showing how and when they'll change from cash *consumer* to cash *generator*.

- Companies must provide a sufficient return on investment to be competitive with alternative investment opportunities. If they don't, they'll have a difficult time getting any investment.

You'll note that these three generic goals correspond exactly to our specific three bottom lines: net profit, operating cash flow, and return on assets. So let's see what an owner or a manager must do to maintain three *healthy* bottom lines.

EIGHT

Managing for Optimum Performance

Net Profit

TOO MANY BUSINESS OWNERS AND MANAGERS GET THEIR financials at the end of the month or the end of the quarter and just glance at them. Maybe they register a moment of satisfaction or a moment of worry. Maybe they breathe a prayer that the next period will be as good or better. But then they put them aside.

Using your financials in this way is hardly using them at all. If you're a Colorado Rockies fan, you don't expect the Rockies' general manager just to check the team's won-lost record at the end of the season and then tell the press that he hopes next year will be better. You expect the GM to figure out *why* the Rockies did as well or as poorly as they did. You expect him to make plans to do better next year. It's the same with business. If you own a company, you want to know not only what happened but why. You also want to know what you can do about it.

The financials prepared by your accountant, in short, are not an end product. They're a work in process. They're a tool. They're a starting point for analysis of your business. The key is knowing how to do that analysis intelligently. Let's start with the income statement—also known as the statement of earnings, statement of operations, profit-and-loss statement, or just P&L—where the bottom line is net profit.

To begin, review the basics of an income statement. The top line is labeled *sales* or *revenue*. It shows the dollar amount of the goods or services you have delivered to your customers and that they have agreed to pay for. (Remember: it does *not* show the cash you have actually received.) On many income statements, the next line will be cost of goods sold (COGS), cost of services (COS), or some other indication of the costs specifically incurred in providing the goods or services your company offers. Depending on your business, these costs may include the cost of goods you bought for resale, the direct labor and materials and factory overhead involved in providing your manufactured products, or the specific cost of delivering your services. (See Chapter 3 for more detail about this last point.) Sales minus COGS or COS equals *gross profit*. Gross profit divided by sales—a percentage—is usually called *gross margin*.

After COGS or COS come several lines of *expenses*, sometimes known as nonmanufacturing overhead or (in service companies) just overhead. We have called these expenses MSG&A, for marketing, selling, general, and administrative expenses. Some companies use shorter terms, such as SG&A or just G&A, while a few companies prefer the term *operating expense*. Accounting standards are weak on terminology; there are many variations on terms such as these, and the variation is greatest on the income statement. But whatever you call these lines, gross profit minus expenses equals net profit.

Net profit is what most businesspeople are taught—and expect—to manage. That's what business school students learn to emphasize. That's what your accountant probably tells you to focus on. So the chances are that you're already looking most carefully at the number that appears on the bottom line of your income statement.

But what do you do if you find you have a profit problem—that your profit isn't as high as you'd like it to be or even (shudder) that there's no profit at all?

Well, you know that the income statement consists of sales minus costs and expenses. So the first thing you check is whether sales are on target. If they aren't, you need to analyze that number further. We'll get to the analysis of sales in Chapter 10, which explains return on assets.

Next, you look at costs and expenses—and what counts, obviously, is not the absolute level of costs and expenses but *costs and expenses compared to sales.* One common approach is to calculate your gross margin and compare it from one year to another. Is it headed in the right direction?

Our recommended approach is to figure out the two key ratios that determine net profit. Divide:

$$\frac{COGS}{sales}$$

and

$$\frac{MSG\&A}{sales}$$

What do those numbers tell you? Unless they're very dramatic—COGS larger than sales, say—the probable answer is, not much. The reason is that you don't know what the ratio *should* look like. Unfortunately, we can't tell you any absolute numbers either. Companies in different industries have wildly different ratios. COGS in the supermarket industry might be more than 90 percent of sales. In an antique or jewelry business, COGS that high would spell big trouble.

However, there are a couple of very good ways to determine whether your ratios are sending you a positive message or a negative one. The first is to compare your company's performance with the performance of similar companies in your industry. Business information sources, such as Robert Morris Associates or Dun & Bradstreet's Key Business Ratios and Industry Norms, can provide you with benchmarking data on key ratios. So, often, can trade associations and trade magazines. The financials of publicly traded companies in your industry are good points of comparison too. Financial people who have worked in an industry for a while generally know what constitutes a reasonable level of costs and expenses for a given level of sales.

A useful trick when you're comparing income statements is to recalculate all categories in percentage terms, that is, calculate what percentage of sales is represented by each line item. Then you can tell at a glance how much one company's performance differs from another's, regardless of how disparate the dollar figures may be. For example, let's go back to the financials of SOHO Equipment, the fictional company we have been using to illustrate our points. You have the seen the income statement for SOHO's first year of operation (Table 6.3). Now take each number on the income statement, divide it by sales, and convert the resulting decimal to percents. The result is shown in Table 8.1.

If Bill and Carolyn, the owners of SOHO, wanted to compare their company's income statement to that of another in a similar industry, they would use the "percents" column rather than the "dollars" column.

The second method of assessing your ratios is to compare your company's performance with its performance in earlier periods. Are the ratios trending upward or downward over three or more years? Let's say you find that MSG&A/sales has been inching upward, for example. Right there you know you may have a problem—and so you have to plunge into the line-item detail of your income statement to find out where the problem might be. Maybe your selling expenses have been creeping upward. Maybe the problem lies in office overhead—rent, util-

TABLE 8.1 Income Statement, SOHO Equipment,
Year 1, Dollars and Percents

	Year 1 $	Year 1 %
Sales	500,000	100.0
Cost of goods sold	350,000	70.0
Gross profit	150,000	30.0
Depreciation	10,000	2.0
Goodwill amortization	1,000	0.2
Marketing & selling expenses	25,000	5.0
General & administrative expenses	130,000	26.0
Operating income	(16,000)	(3.2)
Interest and other expenses	1,000	0.2
Profit before taxes	(17,000)	(3.4)
Income taxes	0	0.0
Net profit	(17,000)	(3.4)

ities, and the like. Maybe your administrative salaries have been rising faster than your company's financial performance will allow.

The key here is to do your analysis intelligently. First, figure out which numbers have the biggest impact on your company's financials. (Percent-based income statements can be helpful in this context too.) Next, figure out which ones are most likely to have changed. If a line item hasn't changed much—or if you know it's right about where it should be—then forget about it. Concentrate on the numbers that might be the source of your problems. You can tell at a glance, for instance, if COGS or COS is a bigger part of your expenses than MSG&A. Whichever is bigger, look there first.

Then too, you have to compare where you *are* with where you *want to be*. It isn't a sin, for example, to run a business for a while with negative net profit. You might be just starting out. You might be investing heavily in growth or in new products. If negative net profit is part of a deliberate strategy—and if you have a well-thought-out plan for turning that negative number into a positive one—then there's no reason to be concerned, so long as you aren't losing more money than you expected to.

Finally, remember that numbers are just numbers and that the real story lies behind them. As you analyze your financials, you'll learn about problems that were solved and challenges that remain. Did COGS go up unexpectedly? You might discover that a key supplier raised its prices—and that Harry, who does the purchasing, wasn't able to find an alternative source until just last week. Is the "postage" line in the expense column spiraling out of control? Perhaps Sue and George in order fulfillment are overusing next-day delivery services. If you're going to analyze your numbers intelligently, you have to remember the human beings and human actions that lie behind them. Then you (and they!) can figure out how to make those numbers move in the right direction. Maybe this is a great opportunity to help Harry, Sue, and George understand what impact their actions have on the company's financial results. Once they understand, they'll be likely to pay more attention to those effects.

We'll show you how these techniques work in practice. But first, we'll bring you up to date on what happened to SOHO Equipment during its first three years.

SOHO EQUIPMENT: THE THREE-YEAR STORY

When Bill and Carolyn Michaels bought the small office equipment business from Kyle Williams, they had some big ideas. They wanted to grow the company. They felt certain that the customer base was larger than Williams had imagined. They were both experienced marketers, and they had several ideas about how to reach prospective customers with their message. But they also knew that the message itself was all-important. They had to deliver fast, high-quality service. If a customer called to order something, SOHO Equipment had to fill that order within twenty-four hours if at all possible. If a customer called with a problem, SOHO Equipment had to solve that problem equally quickly.

The first year went by rapidly, and all things considered the couple was remarkably successful. They began experimenting with marketing campaigns. They took a physical inventory every month to make sure that their records were accurate and that they had a sufficient supply of goods to ensure that fast turnaround. They began to establish close working relationships with their vendors, so that they could get a piece of equipment quickly when they needed it. To be sure, it wasn't all smooth. Bill and Carolyn both found themselves working killer hours. And there were the inevitable glitches. One day, Charlie got lost trying to find a customer's farm on the outskirts of town—and when he stopped to ask directions, the van got mired in the mud and had to be pulled out by a neighbor's tractor. Another day, Claire got an order mixed up in the office, and Donna spent a couple of hours delivering the wrong printer to a customer and hooking it up. That customer was so upset he never came back.

In the second and third years, Bill and Carolyn kicked the marketing into high gear. Bill was sending out targeted direct-mail flyers every quarter. Carolyn hired a telemarketing firm to do cold calling, supplementing her own efforts. They joined the Chamber of Commerce and were asked to give a presentation on how to set up a home office. (It was the best-attended presentation that year, according to the president.) As sales went up, they were careful to keep a watchful eye on expenses—and got everyone in the shop involved in helping to keep expenses low. When the van broke down, Donna got her uncle to fix it. When Claire got sick of taking calls from long-distance telephone marketers, she decided to research the situation herself—and found a vendor that cut SOHO's phone bills by close to 10 percent. The news at the end of Year 2 seemed great. Sales had risen a whopping 50 percent, to $750,000. Better yet, the accountant told Bill and Carolyn that SOHO had turned the corner, earning a profit of nearly $17,000. Once more, the champagne came out—this time for all hands.

As Year 3 came to a close, however, the financial news was mixed. Sales continued to rise, albeit not at the previous year's blistering pace: they were up 20 percent, to $900,000. Once more there was a profit. But the profit this year was slightly *smaller* than last year's, even though sales were substantially higher. What's more, the company was obviously still struggling. None of the employees had seen a raise in three years. Bill and Carolyn were taking only minuscule salaries, which meant they were living off savings.

And then there was the cash problem. Cash at the company was perpetually tight. Thanks to the Chamber of Commerce membership, the couple had been warmly received by the local bank; they had applied for and received a line of credit secured by their receivables and inventory. But in both years they had had to draw on the line, so SOHO was gradually sinking deeper into debt.

ANALYZING THE INCOME STATEMENT

Finally, with the financials in hand for Year 3, Bill and Carolyn sat down to analyze exactly what was wrong. They started with the company's income statements for the past three years (Table 8.2).

They noticed first what they already knew: sales were rising at a good clip. Sometimes this kind of fast growth can put a strain on a company's profits. Maybe that was the case here—or maybe not. Profits turned positive in Year 2, hitting 2.3 percent of sales. But in Year 3, when sales growth slowed, profits were only 1.4 percent of sales. (We call this ratio *return on sales*; it is also known as *net margin*.)

Puzzled, they examined the key ratios on the income statement, shown in Table 8.3.

TABLE 8.2　Income Statement, SOHO Equipment, Years 1–3

	Year 1	Year 2	Year 3
Sales	$500,000	$750,000	$900,000
Cost of goods sold	350,000	520,000	635,000
Gross profit	150,000	230,000	265,000
Depreciation	10,000	10,000	12,000
Goodwill amortization	1,000	1,000	1,000
Marketing & selling expense	25,000	40,000	54,000
General & administrative expense	130,000	160,000	180,000
Operating income	(16,000)	19,000	18,000
Interest and other expenses	1,000	2,000	4,000
Profit before taxes	(17,000)	17,000	14,000
Income taxes	0	0	1,000
Net profit	$(17,000)	$ 17,000	$ 13,000

Right away they could see one possible reason for the improvement from Year 1 to Year 2: the decrease in COGS/sales. To be sure, the decrease was small, only 0.7 percentage points (from 70.0 percent to 69.3 percent). But a 1-point change on sales of $750,000 meant a swing of $7,500—so a 0.7-point decrease translated to an extra profit of more than $5,000.

MSG&A/sales had decreased even more from Year 1 to Year 2—4.3 percentage points, from 31.0 percent to 26.7 percent. That was even more important! A decline of 4.3 percentage points on $750,000 in sales translated to more than $32,000 in extra profit. The improvement in the two ratios made all the difference.

But when they turned to Year 3 they saw a different story. MSG&A/sales continued its downward trend, although the improvement wasn't as great. COGS/sales, however, had started back upward, and indeed was *higher* than it had been in Year 1—70.6 percent versus 70 percent. *The deterioration in profitability was due exclusively to the change in COGS/sales.* If the ratio had stayed where it was in Year 2, the company's operating income would have been better by almost $12,000 (70.6 percent – 69.3 percent = 1.3 percent, and 1.3 percent × $900,000 = $11,700).

TABLE 8.3   SOHO Equipment: Key Income-Statement Numbers

	Year 1	*Year 2*	*Year 3*
Sales	$500,000	$750,000	$900,000
COGS/sales[a]	70.00%	69.33%	70.56%
MSG&A/sales[b]	31.00%	26.67%	26.00%
Net profit	($17,000)	$17,000	$13,000
Return on sales (ROS)	(3.40%)	2.27%	1.44%

[a] COGS: Cost of goods sold.

[b] MSG&A: Marketing, selling, general, and administrative expenses.

Once the problem was isolated, Bill and Carolyn had to undertake the more detailed analysis that would show them where the problem came from. They knew that COGS was rising faster than sales. But was this true across the board or was it limited to only a few products? Poring over the books one evening, Bill spotted the problem instantly. One line of equipment he carried had been growing more expensive, contrary to the trend in the industry, because the manufacturer kept adding more bells and whistles. It was a popular line, and Bill had been hesitant to raise his own prices. But when he calculated the gross margin he was earning on that particular line of products, he let out a whistle of dismay. It wasn't anywhere near as high as he expected to make, and it was considerably lower than what it had been in Year 1 and Year 2.

To check his finding, he toted up all the sales of that particular line and all the cost of goods that applied to it, then subtracted those numbers from his overall figures. Sure enough: without that line, COGS/sales would have continued its downward course. And he and Carolyn would have been looking at a much more profitable year than they actually experienced.

Bill and Carolyn could also see the importance of holding the line on MSG&A/sales, so they analyzed those numbers too—just to see what they were doing right. They could see that, in the short term, many of the expenses listed under MSG&A were fixed. Unless they added another person or expanded into a larger space, the expenses wouldn't vary much with sales. They could also see that Claire's efforts on matters such as the long-distance phone service were paying off.

Of course, the owners of SOHO Equipment had only begun their analysis; they still needed to look at operating cash flow and return on assets. But they had already learned one key lesson: the financial statements provide the big picture. They show you where your company's strengths and weaknesses are. But they also provide the entry point you need to drill down and pinpoint exactly what is behind those strengths and weaknesses. You can move from the big picture to the specific and back again, and in so doing you figure out what needs to be done to improve the big picture.

NINE

Managing for Optimum Performance
Operating Cash Flow

MOST BUSINESSPEOPLE ARE TAUGHT TO MANAGE PROFIT. Very few are taught to manage cash flow. And yet cash flow is every bit as important as profit. For a small or growing company, cash flow is the very lifeblood of the business. If a small company runs out of cash, it dies. For large, healthy companies—companies that aren't in any danger of running out of cash—cash flow is the best way to test the *quality* of earnings. It tells you whether the abstract profits recorded on the income statement are being converted into real money.

To refresh your memory, here's a quick review of the cash-flow statement. The top line is collections from customers. That's all the cash the company received from its business operations. Next come several lines reporting cash paid out—for inventory, for expenses, for interest, and so on. The net of all these lines is cash flow from operating activities or just operating cash flow (OCF). It's one of the most important lines for any business owner to look at.

For some very small companies, OCF may be the same as the bottom line on the cash-flow statement because they're not doing any borrowing or investing. Most businesses, however, have additional lines on the statement. If they have paid out cash for fixed assets or other investments (such as long-term certificates of deposit), those will be listed, along with a summary line labeled cash flow from investing activities (ICF). If the businesses have borrowed money or made payments on a loan, those amounts—just the principal, not the interest—will appear next on the statement, as will any payments of dividends to shareholders. All these last items will be summed up as cash flow from financing activities (FCF).

Finally, the whole statement will be summed up as increase/decrease in cash, or just change in cash. That shows the net amount that went into or out of your company's bank accounts in the course of the year (see Table 9.1).

OK, so what constitutes a healthy cash flow?

As always, it depends on your company's situation. If you're just starting out, you're likely to have a significant cash flow from financing activities—that is, you're getting much of your cash from loans or from equity investments. You may be spending a lot on assets, so you'll have a sizable (negative) cash flow related to investing activities. With these numbers, all you need to know here is whether you're on plan or not.

Once a company is past the start-up phase, however, the *key test of its cash-flow health is its operating cash flow*. You want to hold this number up to the light and look at it carefully. You want to compare it with other numbers to be sure it's moving in the right direction. When financial analysts look at a company, one of the first things they're likely to do is dig up the OCF numbers and apply four tests:

1. Is OCF positive? Once a company is past the startup phase it *must* have positive OCF, except in unusual circumstances. If your OCF isn't positive, you need to find out why—quickly.
2. Is OCF greater than net profit? In almost all cases it should be. Profit, after all, is reduced by allowances for depreciation. If your OCF is smaller than net profit, you'll need to find out why you are not successfully turning your profit into cash.
3. Is OCF greater than fixed asset investment? If so, you're funding your investment internally. That usually indicates a stronger company than one that must rely on outside financing.

4. Finally, is OCF trending in the same direction as net profit? Get out your statements for three years and compare them. If profit is heading up while OCF is heading down, you have a problem.

SOHO EQUIPMENT: ANALYZING CASH FLOW

Bill and Carolyn ran the above tests on SOHO Equipment to see if their company had a cash-flow problem:

*   Test 1: Positive OCF? Uh-oh. SOHO had a sizable *negative* OCF for all three years: ($16,000) in Year 1, ($37,000) in Year 2, and ($33,000) in Year 3. This indicates a potentially serious problem.
*   Test 2: OCF greater than net profit? Hardly. Net profit in Years 2 and 3 was positive—see Table 8.2—while OCF remained negative. Again, this indicates a problem.

TABLE 9.1   Cash-Flow Statement, SOHO Equipment, Years 1–3

	Year 1	Year 2	Year 3
Collections from customers	$470,000	$705,000	$865,000
Cash paid to suppliers (inventory paid)	(380,000)	(550,000)	(675,000)
Expenses paid (MSG&A paid)	(105,000)	(190,000)	(219,000)
Interest and other paid	(1,000)	(2,000)	(4,000)
Income taxes paid	(0)	(0)	(0)
Cash flow from operating activities (OCF)	(16,000)	(37,000)	(33,000)
Fixed asset investment	(0)	(0)	(20,000)
Other investments	(0)	(0)	(0)
Cash flow from investing activities (ICF)	0	0	(20,000)
Borrow (payback)	11,000	21,000	52,000
Paid in (paid out)	0	0	0
Dividends	(0)	(0)	(0)
Cash flow from financing activities (FCF)	11,000	21,000	52,000
Increase/decrease in cash (change in cash)	(5,000)	(16,000)	(1,000)
Beginning cash	25,000	20,000	4,000
Ending cash	$20,000	$4,000	$3,000

- Test 3: OCF greater than fixed asset investment? Well, SOHO had fixed asset investment only in Year 3. In that year its OCF was ($33,000)—a negative number. So it sure couldn't fund its fixed asset investment of $20,000 out of OCF!

- Test 4: OCF trending in the same direction as net profit? Overall, for the first three years, no. Net profit climbed from ($17,000) in Year 1 to $17,000 in Year 2, then slipped to $13,000 in Year 3 (Table 8.2). OCF dropped from ($16,000) in Year 1 to ($37,000) in Year 2 and rose slightly to ($33,000) in Year 3.

By now, you may have the same question in your mind that was puzzling Bill and Carolyn. *How* can OCF ever be less than net profit? How can OCF be negative in a profitable company like SOHO Equipment? How can OCF be headed downward while net profit heads upward? The answer to these questions takes us back to a fundamental job of the business owner or manager: *converting profit into cash.*

Remember a key lesson from earlier chapters. Net profit is an abstraction. The whole income statement is an abstraction. You can't spend an abstraction. You can only spend cash.

Net profit shows the result of only one part of a business's transactions, the contractual part. If you provide a widget to a customer, that counts as a sale on the income statement whether or not you've actually been paid. And the costs associated with providing that widget count as costs on the income statement, whether or not you have actually written checks to cover them.

So what happens if you make a lot of sales but don't collect the money? You might be showing a healthy profit but poor cash flow. *Too much of your profit may be tied up in receivables.*

And what happens if you buy a lot of inventory in hopes of making future sales? You'll have to pay for that inventory—remember that "cash paid for inventory" line—but you haven't yet made the sales associated with it. *Too much of your profit may be tied up in inventory.*

To be sure, there may be other reasons for a poor OCF compared to net profit. For example, you might be paying your bills faster than you need to (and faster than you can collect your receivables). But in many cases the two biggest variables are receivables and inventory. If a company has a weak OCF compared to its net profit, it's often a safe bet that the people running that company are doing a poor job managing their receivables, their inventory, or both.

Fortunately, you have some great tools available to ascertain where the problem lies. All you need to do is look at a couple of other ratios. They'll tell you whether your receivables and inventory are higher than they should be (or are trending in the wrong direction).

RECEIVABLE DAYS

Receivable days is an accounting concept that isn't hard to understand or calculate, and that can be tremendously useful in figuring out whether too much of your profit is tied up in receivables. Receivable days is the number of days, on average, it takes to collect your receivables. (It's also called *days sales outstanding*, or DSO.) You can figure it out from one time period to the next and see in which direction it's heading. First, calculate your average receivables for the time period in question:

$$average\ receivables = \frac{beginning\ receivables + ending\ receivables}{2}$$

Next, calculate how many times your receivables will "turn over" during that time period—in other words, how many times, on average, your receivables will be paid:

$$receivable\ turnover = \frac{sales}{average\ receivables}$$

Finally, you calculate the average number of days it takes to collect your receivables once. For a year, the calculation is as follows:

$$receivable\ days = \frac{365\ days}{receivable\ turnover}$$

Alternatively, you can combine these two steps into one calculation:

$$receivable\ days\ =\ \frac{average\ receivables \times 365}{sales}$$

(If you're working with monthly financials, use thirty days for the numerator.)

We'll do these calculations for SOHO Equipment and see if the company's cash-flow problem is due, at least in part, to poor management of

TABLE 9.2　Ending Balance Sheet, SOHO Equipment, Years 1–3

Balance Sheet	*Start-up*	*Year 1*	*Year 2*	*Year 3*
Assets				
Cash	$25,000	$20,000	$4,000	$3,000
Accounts receivable	0	30,000	75,000	110,000
Inventory	75,000	105,000	135,000	175,000
Notes receivable	0	0	0	0
Current asssets	100,000	155,000	214,000	288,000
Gross fixed assets	100,000	100,000	100,000	120,000
Accumulated depreciation	0	(10,000)	(20,000)	(32,000)
Net fixed assets	100,000	90,000	80,000	88,000
Goodwill, net	15,000	14,000	13,000	12,000
Other investments	0	0	0	0
Total assets	215,000	259,000	307,000	388,000
Liabilities and equity				
Accounts payable	0	50,000	60,000	75,000
Taxes payable	0	0	0	1,000
Other liabilities	0	0	0	0
Current liabilities	0	50,000	60,000	76,000
Long-term debt	10,000	21,000	42,000	94,000
Total liabilities	10,000	71,000	102,000	170,000
Common stock	205,000	205,000	205,000	205,000
Retained earnings	0	(17,000)	0	13,000
Total equity	205,000	188,000	205,000	218,000
Total liabilities & equity	$215,000	$259,000	$307,000	$388,000

its receivables. First we need the company's balance sheet for all three years, so that we have the relevant figures at hand (Table 9.2).

Next, we'll calculate receivable days for all three years (Table 9.3).

Wow! In Year 1, receivable days stood at 11.0. SOHO was doing a great job of collecting its receivables—maybe because customers were accustomed to paying cash under the old ownership. (If most of a company's sales are cash transactions, its receivable days will be less than the credit period.) But Bill and Carolyn changed that policy and gave them thirty days to pay. Sales rose, yes. But as the company grew, its receivables grew still faster, and evidently no one was paying much attention to collection. By Year 3, SOHO was taking 37.5 days on average to collect on its invoices. The cash needed to fund the company's growth was sitting in its customers' bank accounts far too long.

You can see in this calculation the power of a measure like receivable days. If you just look at SOHO's financial statements, you see sales growing from $500,000 in Year 1 to $750,000 in Year 2 and $900,000 in Year 3 (Table 8.2). That's healthy growth. Certainly the net profit bottom line is moving in the right direction overall, though it took a worrisome downturn in Year 3. What's more, you wouldn't think the company would have to worry about its receivables. After all, average

TABLE 9.3   Receivable Days, SOHO Equipment, Years 1–3

	Year 1	*Year 2*	*Year 3*
Average receivables	$15,000	$52,500	$92,500

(Where do these numbers come from? See SOHO's balance sheet (Table 9.2) and write down the receivables line for each year. Add beginning and ending receivables and divide by two.)

Receivable turnover	33.33	14.29	9.73

(In this step, find sales for each year from the income statement (Table 8.2) and divide by the year's average receivables, above.)

Receivable days	11.0	25.6	37.5

(And this is just 365 divided by receivable turnover.)

receivables even in Year 3 were only $92,500—just a little more than 10 percent of sales. Either one of these numbers seems harmless.

But that's why you have to analyze all the numbers together. In this case, what you have to remember is that your receivables are out there *all year long*. Sure, they turn over; but if an average of $92,500 of "your" money is in your customers' bank accounts every single day, there is a significant impact on your cash. That's why a seemingly modest growth in receivables can have a terrible effect on your OCF—and why you have to calculate receivable days to see if that's where your cash flow problem may lie.

So let's say you, like Bill and Carolyn, find out that your company's receivable days are spiraling upward. What can you do? Well, one step is simply to pay more attention to collections. Analyze how long it takes your company to issue an invoice for a sale and speed up the process if possible. Put someone in charge of receivables (if you don't have someone already) and challenge that person to get receivable days down. Get your salespeople involved in talking to customers who pay late. Get involved yourself, particularly if there are one or two big customers that might need a little nudge from the CEO. Examine your credit standards; maybe they have grown too lax, and you're selling to companies that are themselves short of cash. Even with solid companies, you can be more aggressive in negotiating terms as part of the sale. Offer customers a discount for early payment—and enforce it. Establish relationships with the accounts payable people in your customers' offices. (Send them flowers—it works!)

There are plenty of ways to improve your collections process, but going into detail would take us beyond the scope of this book. Half the battle is just knowing when you have a problem, and that's what receivable days shows you.

INVENTORY DAYS

The second most common culprit in companies with cash-flow problems is too much inventory. And once again there's a handy ratio available to tell you if you have a problem in this department. Simply put, *inventory days* is the average number of days between the purchasing of materials and the sale of the product. Here's how to calculate it.

First, figure out your average inventory during a given time period:

$$average\ inventory\ =\ \frac{beginning\ inventory\ +\ ending\ inventory}{2}$$

Next, you need to know how many times the inventory will turn over during the period:

$$inventory\ turnover\ =\ \frac{COGS}{average\ inventory}$$

For one year, inventory turnover means that you sell your inventory that many times in 365 days. Now you want to know how many days it takes to turn your inventory once:

$$inventory\ days\ =\ \frac{365}{inventory\ turnover}$$

Like the calculation for receivable days, this one too can be completed in one step, as follows:

$$inventory\ days\ =\ \frac{average\ inventory\ \times\ 365}{COGS}$$

Bill and Carolyn calculated these numbers for SOHO Equipment, as shown in Table 9.4.

The news is mixed. SOHO Equipment was moving in the right direction between Year 1 and Year 2 by reducing inventory days from 93.9 to 84.2. Then the number rose again in Year 3, to 89.1. Over the three-year period, inventory days averaged almost ninety days—which means that, on average, *the company's goods sit in the store for nearly three months before they are sold.* This might be a fine rate of turnover for a specialized industry such as rare books. For a highly competitive business such as selling

TABLE 9.4   Inventory Days, SOHO Equipment, Years 1–3

	Year 1	Year 2	Year 3
Average inventory	$90,000	$120,000	$155,000
(To calculate these numbers, refer to SOHO's balance sheet, Table 9.2, and write down the inventory figure for each year. Then add beginning and ending inventory and divide by two.)			
Inventory turnover	3.89	4.33	4.10
(This is just the year's COGS, from SOHO's income statement, Table 8.2, divided by average inventory.)			
Inventory days	93.9	84.2	89.1
(And this is just 365 divided by inventory turnover.)			

office equipment it's too high. No wonder SOHO Equipment is show-ing such poor cash-flow results even though it is making a healthy profit!

What do you do if you find that your inventory days are out of line or if you discover that they're heading in the wrong direction?

Naturally, it depends on your business. Retailers and wholesalers have to balance a number of factors. They want to stock what customers need. They can sometimes get good deals by buying in bulk. These con-siderations push them in the direction of holding more inventory. On the other hand, they may find themselves where SOHO does, with in-ventory days that are too high for their particular business (and a nega-tive OCF to show for it). If your company is in this situation, here are some of the steps you can take:

- Be sure your inventory records are accurate. You don't want to be making decisions on the basis of poor information.
- Do a drill-down analysis of your inventory. The inventory may consist of a few fast-moving items, which you must keep in stock, and a lot of slow-moving items, which customers would be willing to wait for. Not all inventory is created equal: ana-lyze it in terms of both cost and turnover.
- Never buy in bulk just to take advantage of a good price while

forgetting the cost of carrying all that inventory and the cash you are tying up.

- Work with your suppliers (or with companies that would like to be your suppliers). How fast can they replenish your stock? These days, many retailers and distributors are connected with suppliers electronically, and restocking orders go out automatically. Using such a system, you may be able to get by with much less inventory than you are accustomed to.

- Work to improve your forecasting ability. The better you are at forecasting, other things being equal, the less inventory you need. Forecasting is a big challenge. But if you spend some time learning to do it—gathering data, making projections, testing them, learning from your mistakes—you'll find you can achieve a huge gain in financial performance.

If you're a manufacturer, you face a different set of concerns. Manufacturing inventory comes in three forms: raw materials, work in process (WIP), and finished goods. Again, not all of this inventory is created equal from a financial point of view. Raw materials inventory is in many ways the least troublesome. After all, the only cost you have incurred is for the material itself. And keeping a reasonable amount of raw material on hand may allow you to serve your customers better. Finished-goods inventory is more important to manage because now it includes all the value you have added to the raw materials. So it costs more to keep all that product sitting on the floor. What's more, it's all ready for sale. All you have to do is get it into a customer's hands, and you're on the way to converting that inventory to cash.

The most troublesome kind of inventory for a manufacturer is WIP. Work in process already has some value added in, so you have already begun to incur more costs. But the inventory isn't ready for sale and indeed probably can't be sold until it's finished. From an accounting standpoint WIP is a cash sinkhole. From a customer's standpoint, WIP is worthless, or nearly so.

The moral of the story? Manage your raw materials so that your stocks turn over regularly. Be sure your finished goods find their way to customers as quickly as possible. Above all, minimize WIP. Analyze your manufacturing processes to keep WIP down. Look for bottlenecks that cause the flow of work to back up. Learn concepts such as just-in-time inventory management, which is designed to minimize WIP. If your financial statements break out WIP, do a trend analysis: track WIP as a proportion of total inventory to see how you're doing over time. Again, there are many methods for reducing WIP, but enumerating them would take us beyond the scope of this book. However, if that's where your problem is, you better know about it. Or, learn an even newer approach to inventory management, called *demand flow*™ manufacturing, taught by the John Costanza Institute of Technology, Englewood, Colorado.

In sum, poor operating cash flow can stem from many problems, but in most cases it's a result of poor management of receivables and inventory. Sometimes poor management of payables contributes to the problem. And of course, it may not be a "problem" at all. If your company is just starting up or if it's growing rapidly, your operating cash flow may look terrible. But as long as it's where you want it—and as long as you have a plan for turning it around, plus a reliable source of cash to keep you in business in the meantime—you don't need to worry about it. The time to worry is when you're running an apparently healthy, profitable business, but you're not turning your profits into cash and you're not sure why.

TEN

Managing for Optimum Performance

Return on Assets

THIS CHAPTER REINTRODUCES THE THIRD BOTTOM LINE—
the one that isn't denominated in dollars.

Dollars are great. The net profit dollar figure shows you whether your
sales are greater than your costs and expenses—in other words, whether
you're making money on your overall sales. The operating cash-flow
dollar figure tells you whether you're converting your profits into cash.
This number—we call it OCF—shows you how much is actually coming into and going out of your bank account as a result of your business's operations.

If you look *only* at dollars, however, you don't have the full picture of
how your business is doing. You don't have all the measures you need.
As your company grows, for example, you'd expect your net profit and
operating cash flow to increase. But by how much? Are they keeping up
with the growth? Are they increasing as fast as they should? If you look
only at dollars, you might think there are never enough—or, conversely,
that the dollar results are better than they really are. Then too, you
know that a company has other objectives besides profitability, such as
maybe protecting and perhaps increasing its market share. How much
profit can you afford to give up in pursuit of these objectives?

To answer these questions, you need ratios. In particular, you need
the bottom line called *return on assets* (ROA), which is net profit divided

by average assets. Most managers find it an incredibly useful ratio, especially when they're looking at results over a time span of several years. If your company is making money and generating cash *and* if your ROA is near the top of what can be expected in your industry, you have a financially sound business.

ROA is important for two reasons. The first is that it helps with the internal financial management of the company.

From a financial perspective, as we have said, the fundamental challenge facing the owner or manager of a company is captured in the acronym SEA: sales, expenses, and assets. Anybody running a business has to make sure that the company has adequate sales and that the sales are growing. Anybody running a business has to watch the company's costs and expenses to ensure that they don't exceed revenues. And, finally, anybody running a business has to manage the company's resources, which accountants call *assets*. The assets include cash, accounts receivable, and inventory; fixed assets such as buildings, vehicles, and machinery; and intangibles such as goodwill.

Return on assets expands a manager's focus to include the *A* in SEA. We saw in the last chapter the importance of managing receivables and inventory; managers' skill at those tasks has a big effect on whether a company can maintain a healthy operating cash flow. But it's equally important to manage a business's other assets. If you were running a machine shop, you wouldn't want half your machines to be sitting idle. It's the same with any kind of fixed asset, whether it's a building, a truck, or a computer system. You want to put your assets to work. You don't want to be in a position where your sales and profits seem healthy but you're really spending more than you can afford on fixed assets. ROA shows whether you're doing a good job of managing your assets overall.

The second reason ROA is important is that it helps anchor the company's performance in the outside world. Owners and managers always need to know what the rest of their industry is doing, and how "our" company stacks up against the competition. Are we pushing hard enough? Are we doing as good a job as our competitors in managing sales, expenses, and assets? Are we as profitable as they are? Dollar figures alone can't answer these questions because industries are usually populated by companies of vastly different sizes. If you're making $500,000 in annual profit, you know intuitively that your company may or may not be more profitable than a larger company with $10 million in annual profits. ROA lets you see how you actually stack up. You don't have to be *big* to be *good*—but you do have to be able to accurately compare your company's performance with the performance of larger companies.

As noted in Chapter 5, ROA is an abstraction. The numerator, net profit, is calculated according to the rules of accounting. Several important elements of the denominator, such as net fixed assets, receivables, and inventory, are also calculated according to accounting rules. Accountants can manipulate both terms, within limits, by choosing different and perfectly legitimate accounting methods. For this reason, focusing on ROA without also tracking operating cash flow would be a mistake.

But it's a bigger mistake to throw out the baby with the bathwater. Although net profit is an abstract number, it's a very good indicator of whether a company is really making money on the goods or services it delivers. And though the "assets" figure can vary somewhat depending on which rules an accountant chooses, the assets themselves are far from abstract. The cash, receivables, inventory, and fixed assets on a company's balance sheet are valuable resources. How effectively a company uses those resources to generate profits is a good measure of its economic performance.

In effect, ROA shows what you are doing with the money your customers, creditors, and investors are transferring to you. As a manager or business owner, you are spending company money for materials, payroll, and fixed assets. You are getting your customers to promise to pay for what you give them—that is, you're generating receivables. You are also collecting on those promises, thereby generating cash. ROA is one of the best tools we have to show how well you're doing at all these tasks.

So what constitutes a healthy ROA? As with many financial ratios, there's no single benchmark, and average ROA varies widely from industry to industry. So the definition of a healthy ROA depends on what business you're in, and of course on whether your company is brand-new or mature. But if you want to assess your company's ROA, there are three good points of comparison:

- For most industries, it's not hard to find out what is generally considered a healthy ROA for companies in that business. If you don't know, ask accountants or company owners who have been around the industry longer than you have. Get copies of the annual reports from publicly traded companies. Check out the financial statistics provided by trade journals or industry associations. Within an industry it doesn't matter how big a company is when you're judging ROA. You might be running a small restaurant, but your ROA should still be on a par with restaurant industry averages (or you should know why it isn't).
- Then too, if your company has been operating for a while, you can make a chart of your own ROA over time. Ordinarily, you expect ROA to increase as a company gets better and better at earning a profit and managing its assets. If ROA is declining—and particularly if you don't know why it's declining—you know you have a problem.
- Finally, you should be forecasting an ROA for the current operating year, and when the year ends you can compare your actual ROA with the forecasted figure. If you don't make your forecasted ROA, that's another sign that you may have a problem.

ANALYZING ROA

And what if you do have a problem? The logic of ROA isn't hard to understand, so it isn't hard to analyze. To calculate the ratio, you first calculate average assets for the period in question:

$$average\ assets = \frac{beginning\ assets + ending\ assets}{2}$$

(Remember that *assets* are always found on the balance sheet, so you'll need balance sheets from the beginning and from the end of the period you're interested in.)

Then you simply take net profit and divide by average assets:

$$return\ on\ assets\ =\ \frac{net\ profit}{average\ assets}$$

Let's say you've found that your ROA isn't up to the industry average or maybe that it has been declining over time. In other words, you have an ROA problem. What might be causing it?

The cause can only be in the numerator of the fraction or in the denominator. If it's in the numerator, you have a profit problem. You need to go back to Chapter 8 and analyze the ratios we explained there. If it's in the denominator, you have an asset problem: your average assets are higher than they ought to be.

Maybe the problem lies with your receivables and inventory. Go back to Chapter 9 and check the ratios mentioned there, receivable days and inventory days. Chart the trends over time. If the problem isn't in these ratios, check out your cash balance. If you have a big pile of cash sitting in your bank account, it will hurt your ROA—and quite rightly, since you aren't putting that cash to work. Unfortunately, there's no handy rule that tells you exactly how much cash to keep in the bank. You need enough cash to meet your commitments (and to let you sleep at night). But you don't want to have "more than enough" because that means that you aren't utilizing the resources available to you.

Anyway, suppose your receivables and inventory are where they should be, and you don't have too much cash. In that case, the problem lies with the other big category of assets, namely, fixed assets. Fortunately, there's a handy ratio you can use to evaluate the problem.

Here's what to do. First, get out your financial statements for the past three years. Calculate your average net fixed assets for each year:

$$average\ net\ fixed\ assets = \frac{beginning\ net\ fixed\ assets\ +\ ending\ net\ fixed\ assets}{2}$$

Then, for each year, calculate this ratio, which we call the *fixed-asset pay-off ratio*:

$$\frac{net\ profit}{average\ net\ fixed\ assets}$$

If the fixed-asset payoff ratio is heading south, you can draw one important conclusion: you have been investing more in fixed assets than you can put to work profitably. Maybe your building is too large, or you have too many trucks or too many fancy computers. (Not every employee needs the latest machines with all possible bells and whistles!) Maybe you spent more on machinery than was wise. If that's your problem, you're not alone. A few years ago, for example, most major U.S. airlines were showing poor returns. If you looked at their financials, you could spot one big problem: too much money invested in fixed assets. The airlines were buying huge new planes—we know it sounds funny to call a plane a fixed asset, but "fixed" just means it isn't a liquid asset like cash—and they weren't able to generate sufficient profit from those planes. So their ROA was lousy. Maybe some of the CEOs cared more about owning fancy new planes than about decent financial performance.

SOHO EQUIPMENT, INC.

Let's perform some calculations on the financials from SOHO Equipment, Inc. and see if Bill and Carolyn have any asset-management problems beyond what we've already identified. First, we'll figure out ROA for each of the three years (Table 10.1).

The calculations aren't too encouraging. ROA was negative in the first year (7.17 percent) because net profit was negative at ($17,000). That was predictable. In the second year net profit rose to a positive $17,000, and ROA didn't look too bad at 6.01 percent. But in the third year, net profit turned down to $13,000, and ROA slipped all the way to 3.74 percent. Bill and Carolyn were using more assets to make less money. This is not a happy situation.

TABLE 10.1 ROA Analysis, SOHO Equipment, Years 1–3

Year	Net Profit	Avg. Assets	ROA
Year 1	($17,000)	$237,000	(7.17%)
Year 2	$17,000	$283,000	6.01%
Year 3	$13,000	$347,500	3.74%

KEY: Net profit comes from the income statement (Table 8.2).

Average assets are calculated from the balance sheet (Table 9.2): beginning assets plus ending assets divided by 2.

ROA is net profit divided by average assets.

What happened? Bill and Carolyn already knew they had a profit problem. In analyzing it, they had discovered that their COGS/sales ratio was heading in the wrong direction, climbing to 70.56 percent for Year 3 (see Table 8.3). They had figured out that they weren't doing a great job of keeping receivable days and inventory days down. They also knew that they didn't have too much cash sitting in the bank because they were always scrambling to pay their bills; in fact, they were projecting a year-end cash balance of only $3,000 for Year 3 (see Table 9.1). But they wondered whether part of the ROA problem they had identified might be traceable to investment in fixed assets. So they performed the calculation mentioned above, net profit divided by average net fixed assets, and charted SOHO Equipment's performance over the three years (Table 10.2).

TABLE 10.2 Net Profit/Average Fixed Assets, SOHO Equipment, Years 1–3

Year	Net Profit	Avg. Net Fixed Assets	Percentage
Year 1	($17,000)	$95,000	(17.89%)
Year 2	$17,000	$85,000	20.00%
Year 3	$13,000	$84,000	15.48%

KEY: Net profit comes from the income statement (Table 8.2).

Average net fixed assets are calculated from the balance sheet (Table 9.2): beginning net fixed assets plus ending net fixed assets divided by 2.

The percentage figure in the right-hand column is calculated by dividing net profit by average net fixed assets and multiplying by 100.

Both numbers were heading in the right direction in Year 2—but both were going in the wrong direction in Year 3. It wasn't hard to determine the reasons. In Year 3 Bill and Carolyn had borrowed more money and spent $20,000 of it on another van, thus adding to their fixed assets. It had been a good deal—the van was only slightly used and the price was right—but profit hadn't risen accordingly because of their troubles with COGS. (The interest on the borrowing had a negative effect on profit as well.) Added to their problems with inventory and receivables, it meant SOHO's financial performance wasn't where it should have been. And the decline in ROA showed they weren't putting their fixed assets to work effectively. Average net fixed assets, after all, dropped $1,000, from $85,000 to $84,000, or a little over 1 percent. Net profit dropped $4,000, or more than 23 percent. In effect, they were using almost as much in net fixed assets to generate less profit.

SOHO's experience illustrates one important point about ROA: it provides a useful measuring stick for small companies to evaluate their investment in fixed assets. Investment in fixed assets should pay off in the form of higher sales or decreased expenses (compared to sales), which is to say it should pay off in the form of higher net profit. To test whether it does, make a graph of net profit over time and a graph of net fixed assets over time. Ideally, both should be rising. But unless net profit is rising faster than net fixed assets—that is, unless the "profit" line is steeper upward than the "fixed asset" line—your fixed assets are not yet paying off financially.

ROA, in short, is the last step in a basic analysis of your company's financial performance. If ROA is declining, a profit analysis or cash-flow analysis may already have revealed the problem (as it revealed SOHO Equipment's chief problems). But if every trend is healthy *except* ROA, then you have a fixed-asset problem. And you can prove it by comparing net profit with net fixed assets in the manner just described.

ELEVEN

Ratio Magic

Analyzing Performance with the Du Pont Equation

T HE CENTRAL THEME OF THIS BOOK IS THAT FINANCIAL statements fit together, like a jigsaw puzzle. Changes on one statement are reflected on another, and if you put them all together into the Financial Scoreboard, you can trace cause and effect. You can see *why* your business's financials turned out the way they did. That's important because your real job isn't just to understand the financials; it's to run the business—and to use financial information to help you run the business better.

What we have provided so far might be called the basic analysis of financial performance. The next step is what we call *power* analysis. Power analysis shows you how the ratios themselves fit together. It shows you how you can use the connections among them to analyze your company's performance still further. The connections are captured in just one equation—an equation that includes many of the key ratios that a business owner or manager must pay attention to. It was first developed at E. I. du Pont de Nemours and is known as the *Du Pont equation*.

THE "SIMPLE" DU PONT EQUATION

The Du Pont equation begins with an insight about return on assets (ROA), the ratio we discussed in the previous chapter. ROA can be broken down into two component parts. Doing so allows you to ratchet up the magnification, so to speak, and gain more insight into exactly where any ROA problems might lie.

The first component if ROA is a number that many companies use to analyze their financial performance: return on sales, or ROS. (The measure also goes by *profit margin,* net margin, operating leverage, and other names.)

$$return\ on\ sales \ = \ \frac{net\ profit}{sales}$$

Get out your company's numbers and check them. Is your return on sales positive and growing? Just as with many other ratios, we can't tell you what a healthy ROS is without knowing your industry. Supermarkets are lucky to make 2 percent ROS. Microsoft made 39 percent in the fiscal year ending June 30, 1999. But you can always gauge your company's ROS against industry averages and against your own performance in the past.

What if your ROS is headed in the wrong direction—or if it's weak compared to your industry? First, look at sales as a pure dollar figure. Are your sales increasing? Are they going up at a rate faster than inflation? If sales are flat or declining, that's likely to be a problem in and of itself, particularly if you're trying to grow the business and therefore you're spending money on costs and expenses. If you are spending money in hopes of growth but your sales are not increasing, you may be in a cyclical trough—or you may be in the wrong business. If sales *are* growing but ROS is poor, you have a profit problem. It may be that your gross margin is decreasing or that your expenses are increasing faster than sales. You can analyze this problem using the ratios in Chapter 8.

The second component of ROA can be figured out with a little ninth-grade algebra. Here's how to do it. We know that

$$ROS \ = \ \frac{net\ profit}{sales}$$

We also know that

$$ROA = \frac{net\ profit}{assets}$$

So we can write a new equation defining ROA as follows:

$$ROA = \frac{net\ profit}{assets} = \frac{sales}{assets} \times \frac{net\ profit}{sales}$$

—or—

$$ROA = \frac{net\ profit}{assets} = \frac{sales}{assets} \times ROS$$

The new term, sales divided by assets, is known as *asset turnover*. It measures how many times in a given period your assets "turn over" in the form of sales. (Remember, "assets" always refers to *average assets* during that time period.) Sometimes asset turnover is also referred to as *marketing leverage* because it shows how much marketing bang you're getting for your asset buck. The ratio measures how customers are reacting to the resources you have invested on their behalf. If a modest amount of assets generates a lot of sales, they are reacting favorably. If a lot of assets generate only a modest amount of sales, customers are voting with their feet—in the opposite direction.

Other things being equal, higher asset turnover translates into higher ROA. In principle, asset turnover can be increased by either of two methods: by increasing sales while holding assets steady or by decreasing assets while holding sales steady. Reducing receivables and inventory, for example, not only improves cash flow (as described in Chapter 9) but also improves asset turnover (assuming the company doesn't sit on the extra cash unnecessarily).

These terms together make up the first part of the Du Pont equation (often labeled the "simple" Du Pont equation in finance texts):

$$\frac{net\ profit}{sales} \times \frac{sales}{assets} = \frac{net\ profit}{assets}$$

or

$$ROS \times asset\ turnover = ROA$$

The first term, ROS, measures the profit you are able to get from your sales. The second term measures the sales you can generate from your company's total assets. Put them together and you get return on assets.

SOHO EQUIPMENT

Bill and Carolyn Michaels performed these calculations for SOHO Equipment and came up with the figures shown in Table 11.1.

The analysis helped them see even more clearly where their problem lay. They could see that ROS declined significantly from 2.27 percent in Year 2 to 1.44 percent in Year 3. They could also see that asset turnover declined only a little in the same period, from 2.65 to 2.59. Their conclusion? Though they would benefit somewhat from better asset management—in particular, decreasing their receivable days—their most pressing ROA challenge was to improve ROS. The analysis under-

TABLE 11.1   "Simple" Du Pont Equation, SOHO Equipment, Years 1–3

	Net Profit/Sales (ROS)	×	Sales/Avg. Assets (asset turnover)	=	Net Profit/Assets (ROA)
Year 1	(3.40%)		2.11		(7.17%)
Year 2	2.27%		2.65		6.01%[a]
Year 3	1.44%		2.59		3.74%[b]

KEY: Net profit and sales are found on the income statement (Table 8.2).

To calculate average assets, refer to the balance sheet (Table 9.2). Add beginning assets and ending assets and divide by 2.

Return on assets is net profit divided by average assets *or* ROS times asset turnover.

[a] If you said 6.02%, we understand.

[b] If you said 3.73%, we understand.

(When rounding and multiplying numbers, the rounded result may be slightly off, but must be close.)

scored the importance of what they had learned when they analyzed their company's net profit, namely, that they could not afford to let their COGS/sales ratio increase as it had.

THE "EXTENDED" DU PONT EQUATION

Managers generally care most about ROA when they're assessing a company's health. It's the most broadly based "return" figure, and it tells you in one fell swoop how good a job the company's executives are doing at managing sales, expenses, and assets. Company owners and shareholders, by contrast, often care most about another measure of return, namely, *return on equity*, or ROE. It shows how much profit they're making for each dollar of equity they have invested in the company.

What's the difference between ROA and ROE? For starters, it helps to remember the difference between assets and equity. *Assets* are valuable resources the company has and uses in the business. The "total assets" line on the balance sheet includes cash in the bank, money the company is owed, the net book value of fixed assets such as machines and vehicles, the value of inventory, and various other items. But somebody has a claim on all these assets, and those claims show up on the other side of the balance sheet. Some of the claims are held by creditors, such as vendors, banks and other lenders, and the government. These are the people the company owes money to, and their claims are summed up in the "total liabilities" line. Other claims are held by the company's owners. They own whatever is left over—the total assets minus the total liabilities. This is their *equity*.

You may remember this as the basic accounting equation:

$$assets = liabilities + equity$$

Despite the financial terminology, it's a commonsense concept that people use every day. If you buy a house for $250,000 and the bank holds a mortgage for $200,000, you know you have $50,000 worth of equity in the house. Similarly, if a company starts up with a $10,000 stock investment and borrows $5,000 to buy a machine, the company now has $15,000 worth of cash and equipment, or $15,000 worth of assets. But it owes $5,000—the bank has a claim on that—so the equity held by the company's owners is still only $10,000.

Of course, you can imagine a company that for some reason has no liabilities—no accounts payable, no debts, no liabilities of any kind. In that case, its assets are exactly equal to equity. Nobody other than the owners has a claim on any of the company's assets. The *difference* between assets and equity, therefore, is OPM—other people's money. If your company has liabilities, as nearly every company in the world does, it is using other people's money to help generate profit. Its assets are greater than its equity.

From the standpoint of financial analysis, the important question about a business isn't whether it is using other people's money, since virtually all companies do. The important question is *how much* of other people's money it is using, and whether it can do so *prudently* and *productively*. A company, after all, doesn't want to borrow more money than it can put to work. It doesn't want to borrow more than it can afford to pay back. Just like individuals, plenty of companies borrow too much and wind up in bankruptcy court for their troubles.

Maybe you have heard the term *debt-to-equity ratio*, which is simply debt divided by equity. This is a useful measure in that it can show when a company is overextended. This ratio is part of another useful measure: the *assets-to-equity ratio*, or total assets divided by equity. An assets-to-equity ratio of 1.0 means the company has zero liabilities. A ratio of 3.0 means it has $3.00 of assets for every $1.00 of equity, or $2.00 of liabilities for every $1.00 of equity. The assets-to-equity ratio is sometimes known as *financial leverage* or the *equity multiplier*. It shows how much you're leveraging your equity using other people's money.

It's the responsibility of a company's owners, or whoever is accountable to the owners, to manage this ratio so that the business remains on firm financial ground. In larger companies this is the job of the CEO and the CFO. In small companies it's the job of the people who are running the business, who may be the owners themselves. If the company is delivering a healthy ROA *and* if these managers utilize an appropriate amount of financial leverage, they can deliver an even healthier ROE. The reason, of course, is that they are using not only their own money but other people's. It assumes that a higher level of assets generates a higher level of profit, which is often the case.

How much is "too much" financial leverage? Financial institutions aside, we have observed that most established companies rarely go much above a 3.0 assets-to-equity ratio. During the 1980s many companies did—and found themselves in financial hot water. Chastened by this experience, financial managers typically tried to get the ratio back down during the 1990s. Companies naturally have to keep their assets-to-equity ratio in line with what lenders expect, so that the lenders don't get nervous. And lenders usually get nervous when any single ratio goes beyond their standard tolerances.

Another interesting thing about ROE is that you can use it to assess any company's performance against any other company's, regardless of the industry. In that sense it's the ultimate financial measuring stick. Average ROE for large American companies as a group fluctuates between 10 percent and 20 percent. In good economic years the average is closer to 20 percent; in bad economic years it's closer to 10 percent. Of course, there are plenty of variations on both ends of the scale. Microsoft's ROE for fiscal 1999 was 35 percent, while a troubled company such as Boston Chicken had a negative ROE. But if your company is in that 10 percent to 20 percent range, you know its ROE is at least adequate.

By now you may have figured out the rest of the Du Pont equation. It looks like this:

$$\frac{net\ profit}{sales} \times \frac{sales}{assets} = \frac{net\ profit}{assets} \times \frac{assets}{equity} = \frac{net\ profit}{equity}$$

—or—

$$ROS \times asset\ turnover = ROA \times fin.\ leverage = ROE$$

This formula, known as the extended Du Pont equation, is handy because it breaks down the ultimate financial goal for business owners—a healthy return on equity—into all of its component parts and helps them understand how to manage each one. Let's review each term in the equation and the strategies associated with it.

1. Return on sales (net profit/sales). You manage ROS by managing sales and expenses. The key ratios you watch are COGS/sales (if you have COGS or an equivalent term) and MSG&A/sales. Almost every company wants its sales to grow. But over the long haul, no company can afford to have costs and expenses rising faster than sales.

2. Asset turnover (sales/assets). You manage asset turnover by increasing sales faster than assets, by decreasing assets, or both. The key assets to watch in this context are receivables and inventory, since these are most likely to vary in the short term. The key measures are receivable days and inventory days.

3. Return on assets (net profit/assets). Return on assets improves when sales rise faster than expenses and/or assets. Chapters 8 and 9 focus on how to manage sales, expenses, and assets such as receivables and inventory. Analyzing ROA—covered in Chapter 10—forces you also to look at your other assets, such as cash balances and fixed assets.

4. Financial leverage (assets/equity). The assets/equity ratio itself is a great tool to show you whether you're taking appropriate advantage of other people's money. If it's close to 1.0, you may be running your business too cautiously. You may want to take on more debt. If it's higher than 3.0, you may be out on a limb. Then you need to take the opposite moves: retire some debt. With financial leverage, "more" isn't always "better."

5. Return on equity (net profit/equity). For many investors, ROE is the ultimate financial measuring stick. It shows whether an investor is better off over the long term investing in this business or putting money into something else. Your company's ROE must be competitive with alternative investments or you'll have a hard time attracting any investment.

SOHO EQUIPMENT

Bill and Carolyn can use the extended Du Pont equation to analyze their three-year performance at SOHO Equipment, Inc. We showed the first part of the formula in Table 11.1. So now all that's necessary is to add the financial leverage terms and figure out ROE for the years in question (Table 11.2).

What does this show? The Michaels already knew the bad news, which was that ROA declined between Year 2 and Year 3, from 6.01 percent to 3.74 percent. The good news, they discovered, is that SOHO improved its financial leverage from 1.21 in Year 1 to 1.44 in Year 2 and 1.64 in Year 3, while keeping the ratio well within reasonable bounds. As a result, ROE didn't drop as much as it might have.

When you're doing this kind of analysis, you need to have all the relevant numbers at your fingertips—not just the equation itself but all the sums and ratios you'll need to understand what it all means. We have developed a one-page summary sheet that we think provides a handy format for this purpose. It shows the Du Pont equation, together with the key ratios from the financials and the three bottom lines discussed in Chapter 5. For SOHO Equipment's Year 3, our summary sheet would look like Table 11.3 on the next page.

TABLE 11.2   "Extended" Du Pont Equation, SOHO Equipment, Years 1–3

	Return on Assets (ROA)	×	*Financial Leverage (avg. assets/avg. equity)*	=	*Return on Equity (ROE)*
Year 1	(7.17%)		1.21		(8.65%)[a]
Year 2	6.01%		1.44		8.65%
Year 3	3.74%		1.64		6.15%[b]

KEY: Return on assets (ROA) is net profit divided by average assets *or* ROS times asset turnover (Table 11.1).

To calculate financial leverage, refer to the balance sheet (Table 9.2). Add beginning assets and ending assets and divide by 2 to find average assets. Add beginning equity and ending equity and divide by 2 to find average equity. Financial leverage is average assets divided by average equity.

Return on equity is net profit divided by average equity *or* ROA times financial leverage.

[a] If you said (8.68%) we understand.

[b] If you said 6.13% we understand.

(When rounding and multiplying numbers, the rounded result may be slightly off, but must be close.)

TABLE 11.3   Financial Performance Strategies, SOHO Equipment, Year 3

Net Profit / Sales	Sales / Average Assets	Net Profit / Average Assets	Average Assets / Average Equity	Net Profit / Average Equity
ROS	Asset Turnover	Return on Assets	Financial Leverage	Return on Equity
1.44%	× 2.59	= 3.74%	× 1.64	= 6.15%

Cost and expense information		Cash flow information	
COGS/Sales	70.56%	Operating cash flow	($33,000)
MSG&A/Sales	26.00%	Fixed asset investment	(20,000)
Balance sheet information		Other investing cash flow	0
Average assets	$347,500	Financing cash flow	52,000
Average liabilities	136,000	Change in cash	($1,000)
Average equity	211,500	Three bottom lines	
Key asset ratios		Operating cash flow (OCF)	($33,000)
Receivable days	37.5	Net profit (loss)	13,000
Inventory days	89.1	Return on assets (ROA)	3.74%
Net profit/average			
net fixed assets	15.48%		

KEY: COGS: Cost of goods sold, from income statement (Table 8.2).
MSG&A: Marketing, selling, general, and administrative expenses, from income statement (Table 8.2).
Sales from income statement (Table 8.2).
All balance sheet information calculated from Table 9.2
Key asset ratios: See Chapter 9, pp. 93–100 and Chapter 10, pp. 105–106.
Cash-flow information: Table 9.1.

If you prepare this summary sheet to go along with your Financial Scoreboards, you'll have all the financial information you need to assess your company's performance for a given time span right at your finger-tips. For example, if ROA isn't where you'd like it to be, you can see at a glance whether you have poor ROS, poor asset turnover, or both. If the problem lies mainly in ROS, you can see at a glance whether the chief culprit is COGS/sales or MSG&A/sales. Create summary sheets for every year of your business's operation and you can begin to spot trends, even without going to the trouble of charting the results. Once you get accustomed to using these, indeed, you'll find that unusual or trouble-some numbers jump right out at you.

PLANNING WITH THE ROA AND ROE GRAPHS

Using financial analysis for planning and projection is covered in the next chapter. But there's one planning tool we want to introduce while

GRAPH 11.1   ROA Graph, 20 Percent (approximate)

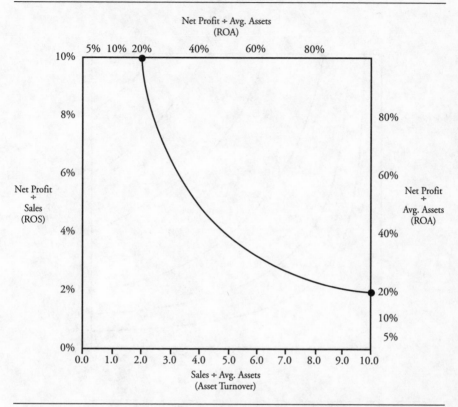

NOTE: From the "simple" Du Pont equation, we know that return on assets (ROA) is the product of two factors: net profit divided by sales, or ROS, and sales divided by average assets, or asset turnover. On the graph, ROS is shown on the vertical axis and asset turnover is on the horizontal axis.

If you remember your high school math, you know you can plot the product of a number on each axis just by drawing perpendicular intersecting lines. For example, draw a vertical line through 5.0 on the horizontal axis. Then draw a horizontal line through 4.0% on the vertical axis. The point where they intersect is one possible point for an ROA of 5 × 4.0%, or 20%.

If you plotted *all* possible points for 20% ROA in the range shown on the graph, you'd wind up with the indicated curve. It shows all the combinations of ROS and asset turnover (within a given range) that can produce 20% ROA.

the discussion of ROA and ROE is still fresh in your mind. It lets you compare your current returns with where you'd like to be—and figure out how to get there.

This tool is based on a simple mathematical fact: if you can multiply two numbers together to get a third number, then you can construct a curve showing *all* the different combinations that would produce that

GRAPH 11.2   ROA Graph, Various Percentages (approximate)

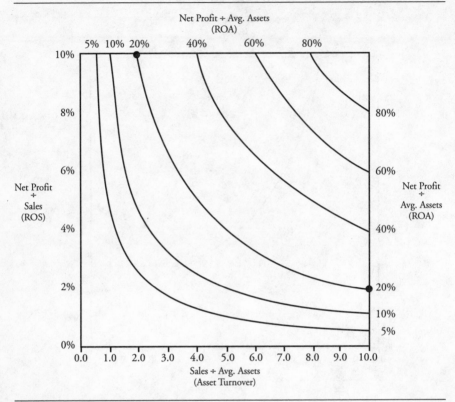

NOTE: Just as you can draw a curve for 20% ROA, as in Figure 11.1, you can draw a curve for any ROA you want. Check it out: imagine a line through 8.0 on the horizontal axis and 5% on the vertical axis. Your ROA would be 40%, and it would lie on the 40% curve indicated in the drawing.

third number. For example, you could produce an ROA of 20 percent with ROS of 2 percent and an asset turnover ratio of 10. Or you could do it with ROS of 10 percent and an asset turnover ratio of 2. Or you could do it with *any combination of those two numbers that multiply out to 20 percent.*

The 20 percent ROA curve is shown in Graph 11.1. You can draw similar curves for 10 percent ROA, 40 percent ROA, or any other number as shown in Graph 11.2.

GRAPH 11.3   ROA Graph, SOHO Equipment, Years 2–3 (approximate)

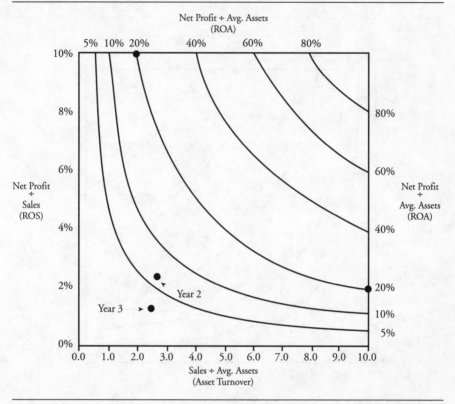

NOTE: This is the same graph as Figure 11.2, but we have added two points indicating SOHO Equipment's ROA for years 2 and 3. Here's the data we used in locating the points:

	Year 2	Year 3
Net profit/sales (ROS)	2.27%	1.44%
Sales/average assets (asset turnover)	2.65	2.59
Net profit/average assets (ROA)	6.01%	3.74%

Now suppose you take this same graph and plot SOHO Equipment's ROA for Year 2 and Year 3. It would look like Graph 11.3.

Say Bill and Carolyn decided that they wanted an ROA of 20 percent. Look at the *shortest distance* between SOHO Equipment's existing ROA and the 20 percent curve and draw it in. (Don't worry about the math; just eyeball it.)

GRAPH 11.4   ROA Graph, SOHO Equipment, 20 Percent Goal (step 1) (approximate)

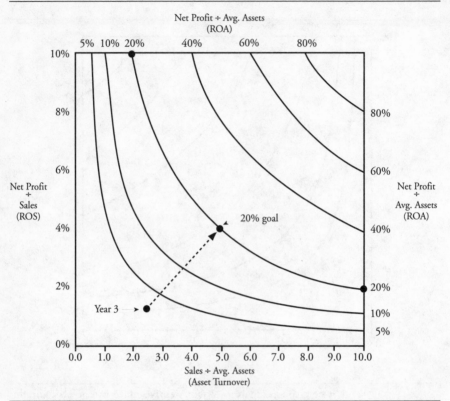

NOTE: To use the ROA graph in planning, start from where you are now. In this illustration, we're beginning with SOHO's Year 3 ROA, from Figure 11.3. Then draw the shortest possible line to the curve indicating where you'd like to be. Here, we assume that Bill and Carolyn want to reach an ROA of 20 percent.

Now look at the point on the curve you have hit. Draw a line down to the asset turnover axis (the horizontal, or X, axis, if you remember your high school math). Draw a line across to the ROS axis (the vertical, or Y, axis). *The quickest, easiest way for Bill and Carolyn to get to the 20% ROA they want is to raise their asset turnover to about 5.0 and their ROS to about 4.0 percent* (see Graph 11.5).

Of course, this is just a guideline. You also have to use good business judgment. If your ROS is high compared to your industry average, you

GRAPH 11.5   ROA Graph, SOHO Equipment, 20 Percent Goal (step 2)
(approximate)

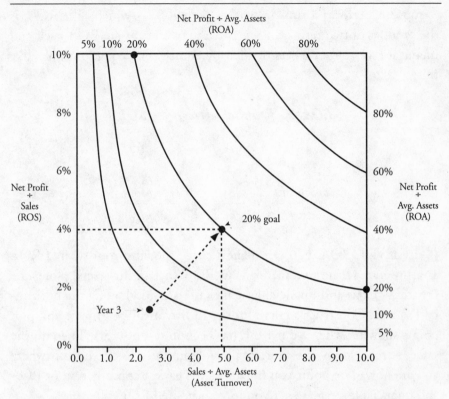

NOTE: Once you have drawn the shortest possible line to the curve, complete the rectangle as shown. Other things being equal, *this particular combination* of ROS and asset turnover is the quickest, easiest way to reach the ROA you're seeking. In the example, Bill and Carolyn would shoot for an ROS of about 4% and asset turnover of about 5.

Of course, other things never are exactly equal, so this is just a guideline. See the text for more discussion.

may not be able to raise it much—and you may have to concentrate on improving your asset turnover instead. But this guideline holds an important lesson. Despite what your accountant might tell you, the best route to better ROA is almost never achieved purely by holding down expenses so as to increase profit. And despite what your VP of sales might tell you, it's almost never achieved by increasing sales while holding assets steady. You need to do both—improve your ROS *and* improve your asset turnover. The ROA curve offers handy guidelines for figuring out where to put your priorities.

You can perform a similar analysis with ROE—which, like ROA, is the product of two terms. In this case the two terms are ROA itself and financial leverage, or assets divided by equity. The equation looks like this:

$$ROA \times \textit{financial leverage} = ROE$$

or

$$\frac{\textit{net profit}}{\textit{assets}} \times \frac{\textit{assets}}{\textit{equity}} = \frac{\textit{net profit}}{\textit{equity}}$$

Just as with ROA, you can make a curve showing your desired ROE as a product of the two factors. Put ROA (net profit/assets) along the vertical (Y) axis and financial leverage (assets/equity) along the horizontal (X) axis. Construct a curve for the ROE you'd like to have and plot points showing where your ROE has been in recent years. Then do the same exercise: draw the shortest possible line to the curve from where you are now. The point you hit shows the easiest combination of ROA and financial leverage to get you to your desired ROE.

For example, if Bill and Carolyn wanted to figure out how to get to 20 percent ROE, the exercise would look like Graph 11.6.

They can see from the graph that the quickest and easiest way to get to their goal—other things being equal—is to increase their financial leverage to about 4.0 and ROA to about 5 percent. Of course, 4.0 is probably too high for financial leverage—but the graph suggests that they might want to increase their leverage as much as they believe prudent.

The key here is to remember what ROE brings to the party: other people's money, or liabilities. The higher your liabilities, the higher your financial leverage and the higher your ROE, all else being equal. You can increase liabilities by borrowing more money. Naturally, you don't want to borrow too much, or you'll put your business in jeopardy. Remember interest expense will increase, so all else won't really be equal. But if your ROA is healthy and your ROE is lackluster, it's a safe bet you

GRAPH 11.6   ROE Graph, SOHO Equipment, 20 Percent Goal (approximate)

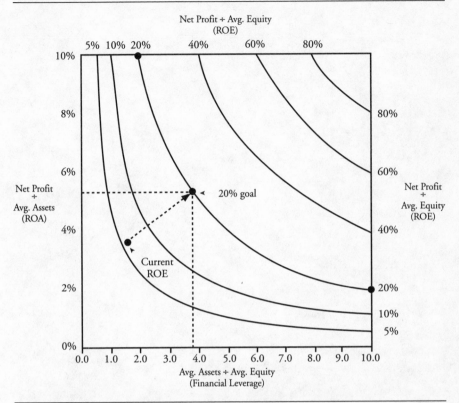

NOTE: This is the same exercise shown in Figure 11.5, except that it shows return on equity (ROE) rather than return on assets (ROA). The marks indicate SOHO Equipment's ROE for Year 3. Here's the data we used in locating the "current ROE" point:

Net profit/average assets (ROA)	3.74%
Average assets/average equity (financial leverage)	1.64
Net profit/average equity (ROE)	6.15%

The diagonal line shows the quickest, easiest way to raise ROE from Year 3's level of 6.15% to a goal of 20%. The rectangle shows the particular combination of ROA and financial leverage that would produce this 20%—ROA of a little more than 5%, financial leverage of just under 4.0.

Again, remember this is just an exercise. Few companies would want an assets-to-equity ratio near 4.0, so this particular combination is probably unrealistic. But the graph does suggest that Bill and Carolyn might want to raise their assets-to-equity ratio, or financial leverage, as much as they think prudent.

aren't taking full advantage of the leveraging opportunities that are open to you. Some judicious borrowing can help your assets/equity ratio and thus your ROE.

TWELVE

Forward-Looking Financials

Setting Goals, Creating Plans, and Making Them Happen

So far, this book has focused on looking backward—on analyzing your company's financial performance to see where the problems lie. But once you have analyzed your performance, you need to look forward and create a *financial plan* that shows, in detail, what you want to make happen in the coming year. The plan should spell out the numbers you expect to see on the income and cash-flow statements for the year and on the balance sheet at the end of the year. In effect, a plan creates the coming year's Financial Scoreboard for your company.

The idea of doing this kind of detailed plan is foreign to many business owners and managers. In fact, many small companies have no plans at all. Their owners run the businesses day-to-day, hoping for the best and taking whatever comes. The problem with this approach is that it puts you at the mercy of the economic elements. Company owners often think that if they work hard and serve their customers well, they'll be rewarded with business. But it's never that simple. If they do get business, will the business be profitable? How do they know? What happens if a competitor opens up down the street? What happens if changes in technology suddenly make the product obsolete or if a whole industry suddenly undergoes a massive change? Think of a bookstore owner

127

faced with the growth of online stores such as Amazon.com or a book-keeping firm whose clients suddenly begin using their own accounting software. Then too, what happens if the economy heads south? If you run (say) a corporate concierge service and all your clients are cutting back on expenses, you may find yourself in difficulty regardless of how good your service is.

Other company owners do a kind of half-baked planning. They eye-ball the revenue figures for the last year or two, choose some arbitrary growth percentage such as 10 percent or 25 percent, and decide that is their sales target for the year. Or maybe they focus on the "bottom line," usually meaning net profit, and decide they want to see a 50 percent increase in net profit. Some even announce these "plans" to the entire company and try to get the employees fired up about hitting the goals.

This approach is also flawed because the goals are not based on reality. Where is that sales growth, for example, going to come from? Which customers? Of those customers, how many are new ones and how many are repeat buyers? You may be the CEO and you may "decide" that your goal is 50 percent sales growth—but why 50 percent rather than 40 percent or 60 percent? Indeed, why do you expect any growth at all? A number plucked out of the air doesn't mean much.

The fact is, neither hope nor faith nor hard work nor all three combined will magically produce a given set of objectives. Rather, some very specific things must happen if your goals are to be realized. If you can't spell out exactly what those things are, you're just blowing smoke—and your employees will know it.

A real annual plan has three characteristics:

- It spells out realistic business goals *and* specific strategies designed to accomplish those goals.
- It takes into account all the interconnected elements of a business, not just one or two.
- It can be translated into hard numbers, as described above.

An annual plan isn't a plan unless you can use it to project an income statement, a cash flow statement, and an ending balance sheet. Ideally, you will be able to show month by month how those numbers will become real.

If you have such a plan, you'll know not only where you are headed but what must happen if you are to get there. You'll have a standard by which to gauge your company's progress month in and month out. If things get off track, you'll be able to spot the problem early—in time to remedy it. What's more, an annual plan is just a starting point. Once you learn how to plan, you'll be able to create best-case and worst-case scenarios. You'll develop contingency plans in case something serious goes awry. You'll learn to manage *to* the plan, adapting your strategies as necessary as the year progresses.

STEP 1: GETTING READY

Before you begin to create the annual plan, you need two sets of data.

The first set provides the context for planning. It's a list of all your longer-term goals and objectives, as described in Chapter 7. You can't create a plan for *this* year if you haven't thought hard about where you'd also like to be three, five, or even ten years down the road. After all, you can't do everything in a year. If you hope to bring out new products two years from now, you have to spend money on R&D today. If you're aiming at taking your company public someday, you may want to invest now in creating the management and accounting systems you'll need then. A longer-term plan isn't the same as an annual plan because you can't specify what you want to have happen in as much detail. But it's indispensable. There's just no point in beginning the annual-plan process until you have a sense of where you want the business to go.

The second data set you need is information about your company's recent history—in particular, full financials for at least three years or (if your company is new) for as long as you have been operating. If you can put the numbers into the Financial Scoreboard format, so much the better. And if you can show the key ratios discussed in earlier chapters as well as the financials themselves, so much the better as well. But however you collect and present the data, the point is simple: you can't figure out where you want to be at the end of this year without knowing the company's performance in the past.

The quickest way to understand the planning process is to see how someone else does it. We'll describe each step and then illustrate it with our fictional company, SOHO Equipment.

As owners Bill and Carolyn Michaels came down the home stretch of Year 3, they realized it was time to do some serious thinking about the future. Running the business had been all they expected—exhilarating, challenging, engrossing. They liked the industry they were in. They liked their customers (well, most of them). They liked the entrepreneurial life. Sales had grown consistently from year to year since the couple bought the company, and there was no reason to think that growth would level off any time soon. In particular, they could see no reason why SOHO Equipment's sales shouldn't break the magic $1 million mark in the very near future.

Long-term goals? At this point in their business life, the couple merely wanted to get SOHO established on solid financial ground, with modestly increasing sales and (ideally) dramatically increasing profits. They wanted to generate enough cash so that running the business wouldn't be such a headache. They wanted to begin taking some money out, starting in Year 4. Basically what they wanted for the next few years was to create a business that could provide them a comfortable living. After that, they'd have to see.

Right now, they knew they were some distance even from that goal. They already had an inkling that the company's financial performance for Year 3 might not look quite as good as it did in Year 2. Cash was still terribly tight. They knew they hadn't really solved the inventory and receivables problem that had been plaguing them. During Year 3, they had had to buy a new van. But since their operating cash flow was still poor, they had gone deeper into debt—and now interest costs were eating into their profits.

Or at least they thought that was what was happening. As they began to ponder their fourth year of running the company, they realized they needed to do some serious information-gathering and planning.

TABLE 12.1 Trend Analysis, SOHO Equipment, Years 1–3

For Year-End	Year 1	Year 2	Year 3
Sales	500,000	750,000	900,000
Fixed asset investment	0	0	20,000
Cost and expenses			
COGS/sales[a]	70.00%	69.33%	70.56%
MSG&A/sales[b]	31.00%	26.67%	26.00%
Net profit/sales	(3.40%)	2.27%	1.44%
Assets & other			
Receivable days	11.0	25.6	37.5
Inventory days	93.9	84.2	89.1
Net profit/average net fixed assets	(17.89%)	20.00%	15.48%
Sales/average assets	2.11	2.65	2.59
Three bottom lines			
Operating cash flow (OCF)	($16,000)	(37,000)	(33,000)
Net profit (loss)	(17,000)	17,000	13,000
ROA[c] (net profit/average assets)	(7.17%)	6.01%	3.74%

[a] COGS: Cost of goods sold.

[b] MSG&A: Marketing, selling, general, and administrative expense.

[c] ROA: Return on assets.

First they assembled data for all three years they had been in business. They compiled their income statements, cash-flow statements, and balance sheets into three Financial Scoreboards. (Year 3 was close enough to the end that they could project their year-end financials with some accuracy.) Then they put together a trend analysis table highlighting the key figures (Table 12.1).

Bill, who liked charts, graphed some of the key numbers (Graph 12.1).

Graphs or no graphs, it wasn't hard to see at a glance where their problems lay. Sales were rising, but net profit had taken a dive, from $17,000 in Year 2 to $13,000 in Year 3. ROA had declined from about 6 percent to below 4 percent. Operating cash flow improved a little in Year 3—it was only ($33,000) versus Year 2's ($37,000)—but it was still a big negative number. In some ways, they could see, things had gotten worse financially between Year 2 and Year 3. It was definitely time for a plan.

GRAPH 12.1   Dollar Trend Graph, SOHO Equipment, Years 1–3

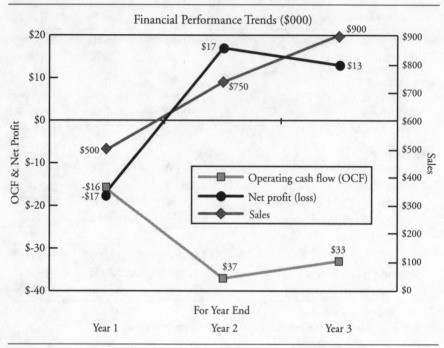

Financial Performance Trends ($000)

STEP 2: PROJECTING SALES

As Jack Stack likes to say, any company's annual plan begins with sales and marketing. Stack is CEO of Springfield ReManufacturing Corp. and writes a column for *Inc.* magazine. He's also a pioneer of the philosophy known as open-book management, which he describes in his book *The Great Game of Business* (Doubleday/Currency, 1992). Our approach has much in common with Stack's. We urge you to begin with a sales and marketing plan—a plan that spells out *what* you expect to sell, *whom* you expect to sell it to, and *why* you expect them to buy. If your company is big enough to have a vice president of sales, this part of the plan is his or her responsibility. Otherwise it's up to you.

As with any plan, history provides a useful starting point. Analyze your company's sales during the last few years. Are they rising? Why or why not? Who are your current customers? Are they expecting to buy from you next year? If so, do they expect their orders to increase or decrease? Depending on your business, you should be able to analyze your past sales by customer, by location, by product, or by whatever other category may be appropriate, and then project your future sales based on as much real information as possible. Some companies survey their customers to see what they're planning on buying during the coming year. Others rely on statistical analysis. Still others simply expect salespeople to stay close enough to the customers so that they can realistically project how much business they will do with each one.

Whatever your method, the key is specificity. You should be able to make statements such as these: "We project an increase in sales of 20 percent because we are opening a new location and we know from experience how much revenue a new location generates in its first year." Or, "We expect sales to stay flat this year because we are likely to lose Customer X, and the best we can realistically hope for is to replace those sales by winning some business from Prospects Y and Z." Good sales plans are built from the ground up, product by product, customer by customer, location by location.

Of course, projecting sales for the coming year is an iterative process. The initial sales goal needs to be scrutinized and measured against the company's resources and capabilities in other areas. If, for example, your market is expanding rapidly, your salespeople may be able to realistically project 100 percent growth in a year. But can your company actually achieve that much growth? You have to ask yourself whether you have the capacity to deliver the increase, whether you have the money available to finance it, whether you can find enough people to hire, whether you are likely to be constrained by supply shortages, whether you'll need to make additional investment in fixed assets, and so forth.

In short, the *process* of doing a realistic sales projection may involve many people. Whoever is responsible for sales and marketing comes up with a proposal, based in reality, as to what he or she can expect to sell. That proposal is analyzed and discussed by people responsible for purchasing, for hiring, for finance, for facilities, and so on. Is it a reasonable plan? If so, what are the likely obstacles to implementing it? Can those obstacles be overcome? Should they be? This process should lead to a realistic sales goal, one that everyone in your company can understand and commit to. The process needs to be completed well before the start of the fiscal year because you will use that goal to develop your detailed plans.

When Bill and Carolyn decided they needed a plan, they turned first to an analysis of their company's sales. Sales had risen 50 percent from the first year to the second year, and 20 percent in the third year. They might not be able to hit 20 percent growth again, they figured, but they still expected sales to rise substantially. How much? Carolyn began pulling apart the numbers. She calculated the number of customers who had bought from them during the previous year. She figured out the average order per customer. She estimated how many of these customers were good for repeat business. Then she estimated the number of new customers they were likely to get from the marketing campaigns they were planning and calculated the new business likely to come in from these customers.

Eventually she came up with a projected 17 percent increase in sales and showed it to Bill. It seemed like a reasonable number—but Bill, ever conservative, suggested they decrease it slightly so they'd have a goal they really felt comfortable with. "Look," he said, punching out numbers on his calculator. "Say we can hit a million fifty—that would be a 16.7 percent increase. Sound good for a goal?" Carolyn agreed, grabbing a big black marker. On the whiteboard in her office she wrote, "Projected Sales for Year 4: $1,050,000."

STEP 3: PREPARING A "BUSINESS AS USUAL" PROJECTION

Ultimately, your annual plan will be based on much more than just this sales projection. You will need to decide whether or not to invest in fixed assets. You'll need to decide how much to spend on R&D, on marketing, and on hiring new people. In all likelihood, you'll also want to take some actions to address your company's weaknesses—for example, increasing profit by reducing costs or improving operating cash flow by tightening up collection of receivables. The plan will eventually reflect all these priorities, not just the sales goal.

But if you try right away to create a full-blown plan that incorporates all these objectives, you're likely to get bogged down in the complexities. After all, a full-blown plan means a complete set of projected financial statements. Since nearly every decision you make has an effect on these financials, it's easy to lose track of which decisions have which effects. What's more, you may miss some obvious problems and opportunities, simply because you're changing too many variables all at once.

So don't try to build a final plan from scratch. Instead, we recommend that you start by creating a "business as usual" plan. A business as usual plan shows you what the business will look like if *nothing changes except the projected increase in sales and corresponding increases in every other line item on the income statement*. Preparing a business as usual plan is a great exercise. It helps you learn the planning process. It also will help you spot problems and opportunities that you may have missed.

Here's how to do it:

First, create a projected income statement. You need to create an income statement first so that you know how much you'd make on the sales increase if nothing else changed. For this exercise, take the percentage increase in sales that you're projecting and increase all costs and expenses by the same percentage. Naturally, key ratios such as COGS /sales and MSG&A/sales stay the same. (You can put down actual numbers for depreciation and amortization, since these will be determined by the fixed assets in place during the year.)

For example, here's the Year 3 income statement for SOHO, together with a business as usual projected income statement for Year 4 (Table 12.2). You'll note that sales, costs, and expenses all increased by 16.7 percent. (We have rounded the numbers so the percent increase will not necessarily be 16.7% exactly for all numbers and have included actuals for depreciation and amortization.)

Bill and Carolyn looked at their business as usual projection and decided that it looked—well, not great. Profit by these projections would be up 23 percent in Year 4, or a few percentage points more than the

TABLE 12.2   Income Statement, SOHO Equipment, Year 3 and
Year 4 Projection ("business as usual")

	Year 3	Year 4
Sales	$900,000	$1,050,000
Cost of goods sold	635,000	740,000
Gross profit	265,000	310,000
Depreciation	12,000	14,000
Goodwill amortization	1,000	1,000
Marketing & selling expenses	54,000	63,000
General & administrative expenses	180,000	210,000
Operating income	18,000	22,000
Interest and other expenses	4,000	5,000
Profit before taxes	14,000	17,000
Income taxes	1,000	1,000
Net profit	$13,000	$16,000

increase in sales. That seemed good, until the couple realized that net profit was still lower than in Year 2! Also, both Bill and Carolyn had learned that profit was only one measuring stick. The income statement wouldn't tell them anything about cash flow, nor about how they were doing in managing their assets.

Second, project the ending balance sheet. Once you have a projected income statement for a year, you can project most of the year-end balance sheet.

This isn't as hard as it sounds. Start by increasing the following items by the percentage amount of the sales increase:

Accounts receivable
Inventory
Other operating assets
Notes receivable
Accounts payable
Taxes payable
Other operating liabilities
Nonoperating liabilities

Debt
Common stock

We have rounded the numbers so the percent increase will not necessarily be 16.7% exactly for all numbers.

Next, remember the accounting rules that determine the other items on the balance sheet:

- Rule 1: Ending retained earnings equals beginning retained earnings plus projected net profit minus projected dividends. To calculate the coming year's retained earnings, in other words, start with this year's retained earnings (off of last year's ending balance sheet), add projected net profit, and subtract any dividends you plan to pay. For SOHO it was an easy calculation. Bill and Carolyn had already calculated their business as usual net profit, and they knew they wanted to pay themselves a $15,000 dividend.
- Rule 2: Ending gross fixed assets equals beginning gross fixed assets plus projected fixed-asset investment. Again, start with the gross fixed assets figure from your current balance sheet and add any investment in fixed assets you plan to make during the coming year. Bill and Carolyn knew they were going to have to buy a new van, so they added in $20,000 for that.
- Rule 3: Ending accumulated depreciation equals beginning accumulated depreciation plus depreciation for the coming year. Same idea here: begin with the line on your current beginning balance sheet, add the amount of depreciation expected this year, and put the total on the Year 4 projected balance sheet. Bill and Carolyn expected $14,000 in depreciation during Year 4, including $2,000 depreciation on the new van.
- Rule 4: Ending goodwill (net) equals beginning goodwill (net) minus goodwill amortization during the coming year plus projected goodwill investment. For the purposes of this exercise, just continue with the amount of goodwill amortization your accountant put on the income statement for last year. SOHO had $1,000 in Year 3, so that's the figure Bill and Carolyn used for Year 4.

Finally, remember that the balance sheet must balance—and so you will need one line that you can "solve for" or plug in to the other numbers so you can make it balance. We recommend you use cash as this "plug" item. It's convenient to do so, and it's a pretty realistic representation of the way most small businesses work.

Table 12.3 shows how the SOHO owners constructed their Year 4 business as usual balance sheet.

Third, create a projected cash-flow statement. Once you have the income statement and balance sheet, it's simply a matter of arithmetic to create a projected cash-flow statement. The Financial Scoreboard shows how the line items all fit together; you just need to do "reverse math" to calculate the values for each item on the cash-flow statement.

For example, to calculate "collections," just add beginning receivables and sales, then subtract ending receivables:

$$collections = beginning\ receivables + sales - ending\ receivables$$

This same rule works for many other items on the balance sheet: just add the initial figure and the figure from the corresponding line of the income statement, then subtract the ending balance sheet figure.

For the following items, however—inventory paid, prepayments, lend, fixed-asset investment, other investment, borrow, and paid-in—you must use a different rule. For these, add the ending balance sheet figure to the income statement figure, then subtract the beginning balance sheet figure. (See Table 12.4.)

The last step in this exercise? Eyeball the plan and see what it tells you. Remember that it is just a first iteration, so there are bound to be problems—but try to figure out what the problems tell you.

With SOHO, for example, Bill and Carolyn noticed right away that the cash-flow statement—and the cash line of $14,000 on the ending balance sheet—didn't look wonderful. In fact, the cash-flow statement showed that they would have to borrow more money and sell more stock to wind up with the ending balance sheet they projected. Even so, the projected increase in cash, $11,000, was tiny, not even as great as the projected net profit of $16,000. Their projected ending cash of only

TABLE 12.3 Projected Financial Scoreboard (Partial), SOHO Equipment, Year 4 ("business as usual")

Balance Sheet, End Year 3

Cash and cash equivalents	$ 3,000
Accounts receivable	110,000
Inventory	175,000
Notes receivable–Trade	0
Gross fixed assets	120,000
Accumulated depreciation	32,000
Other investments	12,000
Total assets	388,000
Accounts payable	75,000
Taxes payable	1,000
Other liabilities	0
Long-term debt	94,000
Common stock	205,000
Retained earnings	13,000
Total liabilities & equity	388,000

Income Statement, Year 4

Sales	$1,050,000
Cost of goods sold	740,000
Depreciation & amortization	14,000
Intangible amortization	1,000
MSG&A	273,000
Income tax expense	1,000
Interest & other expense	5,000
Net profit	16,000

Balance Sheet, End Year 4

Cash and cash equivalents	$ 14,000
Accounts receivable	128,000
Inventory	204,000
Notes receivable–Trade	0
Gross fixed assets	140,000
Accumulated depreciation	46,000
Other investments	11,000
Total assets	451,000
Accounts payable	88,000
Taxes payable	1,000
Other liabilities	0
Long-term debt	109,000
Common stock	239,000
Retained Earnings	14,000
Total liabilities & equity	451,000

140

TABLE 12.4 Projected Financial Scoreboard. SOHO Equipment, Year 4 ("business as usual," $000)

Beginning Balance Sheet		Income Statement		Cash Statement		Ending Balance Sheet	
Cash	3			Cash Change	11	Cash	14
Accounts Receivable	110	Sales	1050	Collections (OCF)	1032	Accounts Receivable	128
Inventory	175	Cost of Goods Sold	740	Inventory Paid (OCF)	769	Inventory	204
Other Operating Assets	0			Prepayments (OCF)	0	Other Operating Assets	0
Notes Receivable–Trade	0			Lend (Receive) (OCF)	0	Notes Receivable–Trade	0
Gross Fixed Assets	120			Fixed Asset Investment (ICF)	20	Gross Fixed Assets	140
Accumulated Depreciation	32	Depreciation+Amortization	14			Accumulated Depreciation	46
Net Fixed Assets	88					Net Fixed Assets	94
Other Investments	12	Intangible Amortization	1	Other Investment (ICF)	0	Other Investments	11
Total Assets	388					Total Assets	451
Accounts Payable	75	MSG&A Expense	273	Expense Paid (OCF)	260	Accounts Payable	88
Debt	94			Borrow (Payback) (FCF)	15	Debt	109
Other Operating Liabilities	0	Interest & Other Expenses	5	Interest & Other Paid (OCF)	5	Other Operating Liabilities	0
Income Tax Due	1	Income Tax Expense	1	Income Tax Paid (OCF)	1	Income Tax Due	1
Nonoperating Liabilities	0	Nonoperating Expense	0	NonoperatingExpPaid(FCF)	0	Nonoperating Liabilities	0
Stock	205			Paid In (FCF)	34	Stock	239
Retained Earnings	13	>>>Net Profit	16	Dividend & Other (FCF)	15	Retained Earnings	14
Total Liabilities + Equity	388					Total Liabilities + Equity	451

TABLE 12.5 Key Numbers, SOHO Equipment, Year 3 and Year 4 ("business as usual")

	Year 3	*Year 4*
COGS/sales[a]	70.56%	70.48%
MSG&A/sales[b]	26.00%	26.00%
Net profit	$13,000	$16,000
Return on sales (ROS)	1.44%	1.52%
Average assets	347,500	419,500
Asset turnover	2.59	2.50
Return on assets (ROA)	3.74%	3.81%
Average receivables	$92,500	$119,000
Receivable turnover	9.73	8.82
Receivable days	37.5	41.4
Average inventory	155,000	189,500
Inventory turnover	4.10	3.91
Inventory days	89.1	93.5
Average net fixed assets	$84,000	$91,000
Net profit/net fixed assets	15.48%	17.58%
Average equity	211,500	235,500
Financial leverage	1.64	1.78
Return on equity	6.15%	6.79%

[a] COGS: Cost of goods sold.
[b] MSG&A: Marketing, selling, general, and administrative expense.

$14,000 was too small—and that was with an additional $34,000 influx from selling the stock.

What's more, the other figures the plan generated didn't look much better (Table 12.5).

ROA and ROE continued to be lackluster, only 3.81 percent and 6.79 percent respectively. Average inventory was headed entirely in the wrong direction, rising from $155,000 to $189,500; inventory days was rising too, from 89.1 to 93.5. The plan showed average receivables climbing from $92,500 to $119,000, while receivable days jumped from 37.5 to 41.4. Evidently it was time to go on to the next step.

STEP 4: PROACTIVE PLANNING

The goal in this part of the planning process is to identify problems to attack and opportunities to take advantage of, so that you can create a plan that will take the company where you want it to go. Again, you can follow a series of steps.

First, update the trend table. Charting your company's performance for the previous years *and* the business as usual projection helps you spot problems and opportunities. If ROA has been headed south, for instance, you know you need to analyze that ratio to see where the weakness lies. If COGS/sales has been steadily dropping, you know your net profit is likely to improve during the coming year as well.

SOHO's updated trend table highlighted the company's problems all too clearly (Table 12.6).

COGS/sales in the Year 4 projection still wasn't under control. Receivable days and inventory days were climbing, operating cash flow was still negative, and ROA was still weak.

As you study the trend table, decide on the *most important* problems or opportunities you should address. This is a critical step because most

TABLE 12.6 Trend Analysis Table, SOHO Equipment, Years 1–4 ("business as usual")

For Year End	1	2	3	4 (BAU)
Sales	$500,000	$750,000	$900,000	$1,050,000
Fixed asset investment	0	0	20,000	20,000
Costs and expenses				
COGS/sales[a]	70.00%	69.33%	70.56%	70.48%
MSG&A/sales[b]	31.00%	26.67%	26.00%	26.00%
ROS[c] (Net profit/sales)	(3.40%)	2.27%	1.44%	1.52%
Assets & other				
Receivable days	11.0	25.6	37.5	41.4
Inventory days	93.9	84.2	89.1	93.5
Net profit/avg net fixed assets	(17.89%)	20.00%	15.48%	17.58%
Sales/average assets	2.11	2.65	2.59	2.50
Three bottom lines				
Operating cash flow (OCF)	($16,000)	($37,000)	($33,000)	($3,000)
Net profit (loss)	(17,000)	17,000	13,000	16,000
ROA[d] (net profit/assets)	(7.17%)	6.01%	3.74%	3.81%

[a] COGS: Cost of goods sold.
[b] MSG&A: Marketing, selling, general, and administrative expense.
[c] ROS: Return on Sales.
[d] ROA: Return on Assets.

companies would like to do many, many things in any given year—boost sales, reduce costs and expenses, introduce new products or services, get some new equipment, and collect their money faster. But if you try to build a plan based on attaining all these objectives at once, you'll lose sight of what's most important for *your* company to achieve *this* year.

Second, allow for longer-term decisions and opportunities. The sales plan needs to be supplemented with other decisions based on the longer-term context. For example, you may decide to set aside resources for a major expansion the year after next. You may want to invest a certain amount in research and development, or in laying the groundwork for a new marketing effort. No company can afford to focus all its efforts on current sales alone. The sales plan, *together with all these other strategic decisions,* sets the parameters for the company's operation during the year. The overall plan says, in effect, *this* is what we hope to accomplish during the coming twelve months.

At SOHO Equipment, Bill and Carolyn had two goals. They wanted to improve their net profit, so as to put the company more solidly in the black. They also wanted to improve their asset management to provide a healthier cash flow.

Third, figure out the key drivers. Once you have identified the problems or opportunities you want to focus on, be sure to identify not only the key numbers on the financials but also the ratios that drive those numbers. Say that your business as usual projection shows a low return on sales (ROS) and that one of your priorities is to increase ROS for the coming year. You then need to analyze COGS/sales and MSG&A/sales to see (1) which ratio has the most impact on your ROS and (2) which ratio is most easily susceptible to improvement. This kind of insight, in fact, is one of the powerful benefits of sophisticated financial analysis: it lets you "reverse engineer" your performance to figure out what went wrong and what must be corrected in the future.

Fourth, "propose" some improvements and pencil them in. If your projections show that you will wind up short of cash, pencil in a lower accounts receivable or inventory number on your financial scoreboard and see what it does to cash. If you like the new cash figure—and if the receivables and/or inventory numbers seem realistic—you can begin making plans about how to boost your collections or reduce your inventory. Similarly, if your projections show a poor net profit, pencil in a lower COGS or MSG&A, whichever is more important to your company. Then begin figuring out whether you can realistically hope to achieve that lower number.

Watch what happens when the owners of SOHO Equipment take this approach.

Bill and Carolyn put their plan aside for a few hours and then returned for another round of figuring. They were ready to pinpoint some possible improvements.

Carolyn, for example, had noticed that their COGS/sales ratio had crept up between Year 2 and Year 3, from 69.3 percent to 70.6 percent. "Shouldn't we expect that ratio to go down as sales increase?" she asked her husband. "Maybe we aren't paying enough attention to pricing when we make our deals with our vendors."

Bill, who negotiated with the vendors, frowned. "We don't have much clout with them. And we certainly don't have the cash available to take advantage of any discounts for early payment."

"I know," said Carolyn. "Still, suppose we could get the ratio down just a little, say, to the Year 2 level. Small changes make a difference when you're looking at big numbers—and this is a big number on our income statement." She punched some figures into the calculator. "If we could just get back to 69.3 percent, that would give us an additional $12,000 in net profit, or a total of $28,000. And if we can hold MSG&A expenses to the same 26.0 percent ratio as before, we can nearly double our return on sales, to 2.67 percent." (See Table 12.7).

Bill brightened. "That's not much, is it? I think we *can* do that. And with our increase in sales, it shouldn't be hard to hold MSG&A to the same ratio as before. Maybe we can even afford to give our people a small raise. They certainly deserve it."

Using these numbers, Bill and Carolyn then projected a new income statement for Year 4 (See Table 12.8 on page 146. We label it the "proactive" income statement, to distinguish it from the "business as usual" income statement for Year 4 shown in Table 12.2 on page 136.)

TABLE 12.7   Income Statement, SOHO Equipment, Year 4 (partial)

	Business As Usual	Proactive
Sales	$1,050,000	$1,050,000
Cost of goods sold	740,000	728,000
Gross profit	310,000	322,000
Net profit	16,000	28,000
Return on sales (ROS)	1.52%	2.67%

"Wow!" exclaimed Carolyn. "We can *make* that $28,000 in net profit. That's on the right track."

The owners of SOHO also wanted to improve their cash flow. They knew that the key numbers, for them, were inventory and receivables—but they weren't sure what level was realistic. "Look at the accounts receivable line on the business-as-usual projection," Bill said, as he studied Table 12.4. "It shows $128,000 in ending receivables. That's way high. Suppose we projected that at $100,000." Bill began working the calculator's keys. "Hmm," he said. "If ending receivables are $100,000, then average receivables for Year 4 are $105,000." Rearranging the equation for receivable days (page 93), he came up with this calculation:

$$receivable\ days = \frac{average\ receivables \times 365}{sales}$$

With projected sales of $1,050,000 and average receivables of $105,000, the equation produced a figure of 36.5 for receivable days. "That's only a little better than last year," he said. "We can do better than that."

In the next try, he cut projected ending receivables drastically—and wound up with a receivable days figure even lower than Year 2. "Sorry," said Carolyn. "That's too unrealistic. How can we possibly get our receivable days down that much?"

TABLE 12.8   Income Statement, SOHO Equipment,
Year 4 (proactive)

Sales	$1,050,000
Cost of goods sold	728,000
Gross profit	322,000
Depreciation	14,000
Goodwill amortization	1,000
Marketing & selling expenses	63,000
General & administrative expenses	210,000
Operating income	34,000
Interest and other expenses	5,000
Profit before taxes	29,000
Income taxes	1,000
Net profit	$ 28,000
Return on sales (ROS)	2.67%

After two more tries, the couple came up with a figure they agreed on: projected ending receivables of $82,000, translating into receivable days of 33.4—a modest improvement on Year 3's number of 37.5 but not impossibly ambitious. "We just have to collect our receivables an average of four days sooner," said Bill. "We can *do* that—and knowing what the goal is will give us a target to shoot for. We can monitor it each month."

The next challenge was inventory. SOHO's business as usual projections showed ending inventory climbing drastically, to $204,000. Bill had been talking with the manufacturer of the company's best-selling computer, however, and he had an idea. "You know how Dell Computer builds computers to a customer's order? Well, the guys we buy from are implementing a similar build-to-order program, and they're willing to work with their distributors on it. Instead of shipping us a bunch of machines that we have to stock, they'll ship each computer on demand—and much of the customization will already be done when it arrives here."

Bill made some calculations with his pencil. "Those computers accounted for a significant fraction of our inventory. If we can take advantage of this new program, we can get inventory down significantly in the next year even with our projected increase in sales."

Carolyn, meanwhile, was punching in numbers of her own (using the formula for inventory days on page 97). "Hey," she said. "Check this out. Ending inventory in the business as usual projection is $204,000 [Table 12.4]. But if we can get our ending inventory down to $161,000, then our average inventory is $168,000—and our inventory days are 84.2. That's exactly what inventory days were in Year 2—and it's one heckuva lot better than we were looking at in our business as usual projection."

"That's doable," said Bill. "But let's say we can achieve all those goals—what effect will it have on our Financial Scoreboard?"

The couple entered the numbers. Taking their revised income statement, they created a new projected ending balance sheet—except this time they put in their new numbers for accounts receivable and inventory. They noticed that nothing changed except those line items, along with the retained earnings line (which reflected the projected increase in net profit). Hurrying, Bill went on to the next step, which was to add up liabilities and equity, then subtract all the assets listed. That, he knew, would give them the ending cash figure for the year. "Carolyn," he said. "Look at this."

Could it be real? They would wind up with $115,000 in cash (See Table 12.9 on page 148.).

Bill began to create a projected Financial Scoreboard for Year 4 (See Table 12.10 on page 149.). "It's real, all right. We'd be showing an operating cash flow of $98,000, and a total change in cash of $112,000." These were numbers the couple could really live with.

Bill and Carolyn realized that all the planning was based on some big challenges. They had to figure out how to reduce the COGS/sales ratio to where it had been in the past. That meant some tough negotiating with vendors. They had to try out the new program offered by the computer manufacturer, and keep an eye on how it affected their inventory numbers. They had to get on top of collections—the cash flow statement showed collections of $1,078,000, or more than their projected sales. Still, they were heartened by the fact that receivable days were decreasing only modestly. If they could just get the money in the door a *little* faster, it would have the desired effect.

TABLE 12.9   Ending Balance Sheet, SOHO
Equipment, Year 4 (proactive)

Assets	
Cash and cash equivalents	$115,000
Accounts receivable	82,000
Inventory	161,000
Notes receivable	0
Current assets	358,000
Gross fixed assets	140,000
Accumulated depreciation	(46,000)
Net fixed assets	94,000
Goodwill, net	11,000
Other investments	0
Total assets	463,000
Liabilities and equity	
Accounts payable	88,000
Taxes payable	1,000
Other liabilities	0
Current liabilities	89,000
Long-term debt	109,000
Total liabilities	198,000
Common stock	239,000
Retained earnings	26,000
Total equity	265,000
Total liabilities & equity	$463,000

But if they could reach those goals, they would be well on their way to having a solid, viable business—one that was actually making money and generating significant amounts of cash. ROA in the projection was 6.58 percent, and ROE was up to 11.59 percent.

STEP 5: REFINING THE PLAN

Once you have a plan that looks good—that seems workable and gets you on the path toward achieving your objectives—you may want to refine it in various ways, as well as develop alternative plans allowing for different inputs and outcomes. Here are three kinds of "next steps" to consider.

TABLE 12.10 Financial Scoreboard, SOHO Equipment, Year 4 (proactive, $000)

Beginning Balance Sheet		Income Statement		Cash Statement		Ending Balance Sheet	
3	Cash	1050	Sales	112	Cash Change	115	Cash
110	Accounts Receivable	728	Cost of Goods Sold	1078	Collections (OCF)	82	Accounts Receivable
175	Inventory			714	Inventory Paid (OCF)	161	Inventory
0	Other Operating Assets			0	Prepayments (OCF)	0	Other Operating Assets
0	Notes Receivable–Trade			0	Lend (Receive) (OCF)	0	Notes Receivable–Trade
120	Gross Fixed Assets			20	Fixed Asset Investment (ICF)	140	Gross Fixed Assets
32	Accumulated Depreciation	14	Depreciation+Amortization			46	Accumulated Depreciation
88	Net Fixed Assets					94	Net Fixed Assets
12	Other Investments	1	Intangible Amortization	1	Other Investment (ICF)	11	Other Investments
388	Total Assets					463	Total Assets
75	Accounts Payable	273	MSG&A Expense	260	Expense Paid (OCF)	88	Accounts Payable
94	Debt			15	Borrow (Payback) (FCF)	109	Debt
0	Other Operating Liabilities	5	Interest & Other Expenses	5	Interest & Other Paid (OCF)	0	Other Operating Liabilities
1	Income Tax Due	1	Income Tax Expense	1	Income Tax Paid (OCF)	1	Income Tax Due
0	Nonoperating Liabilities	0	Nonoperating Expense	0	NonoperatingExpPaid(FCF)	0	Nonoperating Liabilities
205	Stock			34	Paid In (FCF)	239	Stock
13	Retained Earnings	28	>>>Net Profit	15	Dividend & Other (FCF)	26	Retained Earnings
388	Total Liabilities + Equity	6.58%	>>>Return on Assets	98	>>>Operating Cash Flow	463	Total Liabilities + Equity

First, consider your options. If the plan shows your company generating profit and cash, as the new SOHO plan does, you have some choices that you might not otherwise have had. For example, the scoreboard above still shows SOHO selling stock and borrowing money—then winding up with a sizable pile of cash at the end of the year. Bill and Carolyn might choose to do that, just to have a cash cushion. But they also might choose to forgo the stock sale and the borrowing and wind up with less cash. They might also choose to pay down more of their debt. That's the great virtue of planning: it shows what's possible.

Second, prepare best-case, worst-case, and expected scenarios. Any plan incorporates numerous assumptions about what will stay steady and what will change. So once you have developed a plan that addresses your problems and opportunities and seems realistic, do another that incorporates your most optimistic assumptions about how you'll do during the coming year, and still another that incorporates your most pessimistic assumptions. You may be surprised by how different they look. However the two turn out, they provide boundaries, so to speak, on your projections. The worst-case scenario in particular shows you how bad things can get. It will tell you whether (or how easily) your business can survive if your worst fears about the marketplace or the economy are realized.

Third, play "what if." Best-case and worst-case plans are *generalized* plans. They assume that things go very well or very poorly throughout the business. A what-if plan is different; it takes a single variable and assesses its effects. What if we spend $20,000 on another new machine? What if we move to a new building? What if we lose our biggest customer? What if sales on our new product really take off? Each of these possible events will have financial ramifications—and these ramifications can be estimated and incorporated in a financial plan. Once you spell them out in this way, you'll be able to see what the consequences are likely to be on the business as a whole.

Fourth, talk to your accountant about taxes. The projection and planning scenarios above don't take taxes into account. As we explained earlier in this book, tax accounting can often look quite different from managerial accounting because accountants often employ a variety of legal methods designed to reduce a company's bottom line and thus its taxable profit. Tax considerations are beyond the scope of this book, but if you are projecting a taxable net profit, you should discuss the tax implications with the person who will be preparing your tax returns.

STEP 6: IMPLEMENTING THE PLAN

Once you have a twelve-month plan, it usually isn't hard to divide it into twelve monthly plans. Figure out any seasonal variations that are peculiar to your business—heavy sales in the summertime, for example, or around the holiday season—and allow for them. Determine the scheduling for any major expenses that don't occur each month. With these estimates in hand, you can prepare income statements, cash-flow statements, and balance sheets for every month (or at least every quarter) of the year. You'll have a plan for each time period that lets you see how you're doing as you go along.

This plan should never change. That does not mean, however, that you should always stick to it or that you can't take advantage of opportunities that arise during the year.

In business, circumstances always turn out to be different from what you expected. Your plans may turn out to be unrealistic. Some new threat or opportunity appears on the horizon, and you decide to take action that you couldn't have predicted before the year began. However, if you change your plan every time circumstances change, you'll have no benchmark, no reference point. You won't know whether what you're doing now is turning out better or worse than if you stuck to your plan. You also won't know at the end of the year how good a job you did at planning because the original plan will be long gone.

So once the plan is made, set it in stone. If circumstances change significantly, create a new set of numbers for the rest of the year—call them "projections" or "opinions" or something else—and benchmark your performance against *both* these opinions and the original plan.

One last comment on planning. If you run a very small company, it isn't hard to share your plans with your employees. In fact, you'll probably be bouncing ideas off one another and coming up with ideas for implementing the plan together. In a larger company, you may want to involve people in a more formal planning process. Jack Stack and others have pioneered this approach; he calls it *high-involvement planning*. It's based on a simple observation about people—they pitch in with more enthusiasm to attain goals that they understand and have had a hand in setting. The entire sales force and marketing staff can take part in the discussions that lead to the sales plan. The CEO can lead discussions among employees about the company's longer-term objectives and about how this year's plan will take the company in the right direction. Teams of employees can focus on individual problems and come up with proposals for how to address them.

However you do it, planning is a key to business success. It's what allows you to translate your financial *understanding* into better financial *performance*.

Epilogue

THIS BOOK IS ABOUT FINANCIAL STATEMENTS—THE NUM-bers of business. The financials aren't the only numbers you check when you're running a company, of course, but they are among the most important. Financial numbers help you know what's going on. They allow you to identify and analyze problems. They let you plan effectively, and they tell you how you're doing as you implement your plans. The book is about understanding these numbers and using them as you run your business. That's why we called it *Managing by the Numbers*.

In closing, we want to add a final word of encouragement, a word of caution—and a suggestion about how to build some excitement and fun into managing by the numbers.

Encouragement first. If you have read this book straight through, your head may be swimming. Terms like *amortization* and *receivables* and *investing cash flow* may be cascading through your brain, with or without definitions attached. You may be a little fuzzy on how to calculate ratios such as receivable days. You may not remember the exact terms of the Du Pont equation. The "power analysis" of the last couple of chapters—for example, using the Financial Scoreboard to project the coming year's income statement, cash-flow statement, and year-end balance sheet—may seem like an exercise in differential calculus.

Trust us: none of this stuff is as hard as it first seems. The vocabulary does take some getting used to, but you'll soon grow familiar with it. As for the skills themselves, they're like any new set of skills you acquire: you'll need to practice. But the calculations are no harder than the ones you learned in eighth-grade math. (You mastered those once; you can do it again!) We have seen literally thousands of business owners and managers—including many who described themselves as "math phobic"—who learned to use these tools and techniques to build stronger companies.

Just don't expect yourself to get up to speed right away. Take a month to familiarize yourself with your own company's financials, so that you really understand what each line item means. Take another month to try putting the information into your own Financial Scoreboard, so you can see how all the numbers fit together. Spend a third month doing nothing but simple analysis of your financials. Plot trends. Calculate ratios such as receivable days. (You'll find all the ratios in Appendix 4.)

By the end of three months, we predict, you'll be running all kinds of numbers, just to see what they can tell you. In another three months you'll be learning to put them into plans and projections. If you're a numbers whiz, of course, you'll get up to speed even faster. But regardless of how long it takes, you'll have a big incentive to do the learning—because the more you learn, the better you'll be able to run your business.

Now for that word of caution. It's easy to misunderstand a phrase like "managing by the numbers," and it's easy to get so caught up in counting the trees that you forget about the forest.

If you followed business through the 1980s, you probably heard critics of all stripes attacking business managers for paying *too much* attention to the numbers. American executives managed their companies to satisfy Wall Street, the critics charged, which meant that they focused exclusively on short-term earnings growth. They had to "make the numbers" or be punished by the stock market. Meanwhile, so it was said, Japanese managers focused on long-term objectives like new-product development and increasing market share. They weren't so obsessed with the numbers.

In the early 1990s, Prof. Robert S. Kaplan of the Harvard Business School and David P. Norton developed a framework they termed the "balanced scorecard." Their objective was specifically to help companies develop metrics that went beyond the traditional financial statements. A balanced scorecard might include measures such as customer satisfaction or the rate of new-product development. The professors' idea was that financial statements *alone* didn't give managers a sufficient picture of their companies' strengths and weaknesses.

The fact is, company managers *can* be obsessed with the financials, just as they can be obsessed with sales or cost cutting or any other part of running a company. Managers of publicly traded companies may indeed focus on quarterly earnings to an unhealthy extent. It is possible to manage by the numbers, especially *short-term* numbers, and forget about everything else.

Obviously, we're not advocating that you focus on the financials to the exclusion of everything else that's important about running the business. You need to have good products, good people, good marketing efforts, and so forth. Nor are we arguing that you should do everything possible to maximize your financial performance in any given year. There may be plenty of good reasons for sacrificing short-term financial objectives while you do something that's even more important for your business, like building market share. Only you can make that call. Only you can balance your short-term goals with your longer-term ones. We just want you to understand the financial dimension of your business backward and forward, so that you can utilize financial tools to help you achieve your objectives.

Finally, we'd like to suggest something important about the whole idea of managing by the numbers. Numbers can build excitement, even fun, into your business.

At first glance, you might think that's an odd idea. "Managing by the numbers" sounds dry, even bloodless, as if we expect you to study columns of figures night and day and forget about the people who make the business go—your colleagues, your employees, your customers, your suppliers. Now and then you'll hear of a big-business executive who supposedly scrutinizes financial reports and makes instant decisions purely on the basis of the numbers, without regard to any other consideration. (Rightly or wrongly, the legendary Harold Geneen of ITT had that reputation.)

But think about competitive sports for a moment. Competitive sports are indisputably governed by numbers. Scores. Times. Percentages. Averages. Sports aren't dry and bloodless: quite the opposite. People cheer and yell and jump up and down just to see which team can rack up better numbers. It goes to show that numbers themselves aren't dry or bloodless. Numbers are just tools; they're just measures. What matters is the activity that the numbers reflect. And the activities we call business can be every bit as exciting as sports. What's more challenging than to establish goals and track your progress in achieving them? In business, moreover, it matters whether you achieve your goals. When a business succeeds, it generates wealth, creates jobs, and provides products and services that people need. A growing, profitable business means more opportunity for everyone.

So here's a suggestion: as you learn to track your financial performance and set financial goals, get everyone involved. Share what you've learned about finance with the others who work in your company. Figure out together your company's goals for net profit, operating cash flow, and return on assets. (Alternatively, if it makes more sense for your business, you can focus on some of the numbers that drive financial performance, such as gross profit or number of hours billed.) Then put the goals up on a whiteboard or an intranet, and chart how you're doing every week, month, or quarter.

It won't be long before the business itself becomes a kind of game. At some companies, people even establish betting pools on when they'll hit their profit targets. And when they do, there's whooping and hollering and celebrating—just as if they were playing a sport. Managing in this way adds fun and excitement to the workplace. It has another benefit as well: once people begin to understand how what they do affects the numbers, they'll figure out ways to improve their performance. And when everyone in a company is worrying about meeting or beating their financial goals, the odds are good that they'll succeed. "It's easy to stop one guy," says Jack Stack of Springfield ReManufacturing Corp. "But it's pretty hard to stop a hundred."

So we hope you have had a great time with this book, and we hope you have a great time learning to manage by the numbers. We hope it helps you build a stronger company. We hope it helps you achieve your goals. And we hope you have plenty of fun along the way.

Appendix 1

SOHO Equipment:
The Complete Financials

TABLE A1.1 Balance Sheet (Start Up and Ending)

Balance Sheet	Start-up	Year 1	Year 2	Year 3	Year 4 Business as Usual	Year 4 Proactive/ Realistic
Assets						
Cash	$25,000	$20,000	$4,000	$3,000	$14,000	$115,000
Accounts receivable	0	30,000	75,000	110,000	128,000	82,000
Inventory	75,000	105,000	135,000	175,000	204,000	161,000
Notes receivable	0	0	0	0	0	0
Current assets	100,000	155,000	214,000	288,000	346,000	358,000
Gross fixed assets	100,000	100,000	100,000	120,000	140,000	140,000
Accumulated depreciation	0	(10,000)	(20,000)	(32,000)	(46,000)	(46,000)
Net fixed assets	100,000	90,000	80,000	88,000	94,000	94,000
Goodwill, net	15,000	14,000	13,000	12,000	11,000	11,000
Other investments	0	0	0	0	0	0
Total assets	215,000	259,000	307,000	388,000	451,000	463,000
Liabilities and Equity						
Accounts payable	0	50,000	60,000	75,000	88,000	88,000
Taxes payable	0	0	0	1,000	1,000	1,000
Other liabilities	0	0	0	0	0	0
Current liabilities	0	50,000	60,000	76,000	89,000	89,000
Long-term debt	10,000	21,000	42,000	94,000	109,000	109,000
Total liabilities	10,000	71,000	102,000	170,000	198,000	198,000
Common stock	205,000	205,000	205,000	205,000	239,000	239,000
Retained earnings	0	(17,000)	0	13,000	14,000	26,000
Total equity	205,000	188,000	205,000	218,000	253,000	265,000
Total liabilities & equity	$215,000	$259,000	$307,000	$388,000	$451,000	$463,000

TABLE A1.2 Income Statement and Cash-Flow Statement

Income Statement	Year 1	Year 2	Year 3	Year 4 Business as Usual	Year 4 Proactive/ Realistic
Sales	$500,000	$750,000	$900,000	$1,050,000	$1,050,000
Cost of goods sold	350,000	520,000	635,000	740,000	728,000
Gross profit	150,000	230,000	265,000	310,000	322,000
Depreciation	10,000	10,000	12,000	14,000	14,000
Goodwill amortization	1,000	1,000	1,000	1,000	1,000
Marketing & selling expenses	25,000	40,000	54,000	63,000	63,000
General & administrative expenses	130,000	160,000	180,000	210,000	210,000
Operating income	(16,000)	19,000	18,000	22,000	34,000
Interest and other expenses	1,000	2,000	4,000	5,000	5,000
Profit before taxes	(17,000)	17,000	14,000	17,000	29,000
Income taxes	0	0	1,000	1,000	1,000
Net profit	(17,000)	17,000	13,000	16,000	28,000

(continued)

TABLE A1.2 (continued)

Cash-Flow Statement	Year 1	Year 2	Year 3	Year 4 Business as Usual	Year 4 Proactive/ Realistic
Collections from customers	470,000	705,000	865,000	1,032,000	1,078,000
Cash paid to suppliers (inventory paid)	(380,000)	(550,000)	(675,000)	(769,000)	(714,000)
Expenses paid (MSG&A paid)	(105,000)	(190,000)	(219,000)	(260,000)	(260,000)
Interest and other paid	(1,000)	(2,000)	(4,000)	(5,000)	(5,000)
Income taxes paid	0	0	0	(1,000)	(1,000)
Cash flow from operating activities (OCF)	(16,000)	(37,000)	(33,000)	(3,000)	98,000
Fixed asset investment	0	0	(20,000)	(20,000)	(20,000)
Other investments	0	0	0	0	0
Cash flow from investing activities (ICF)	0	0	(20,000)	(20,000)	(20,000)
Borrow (payback)	11,000	21,000	52,000	15,000	15,000
Paid in/paid out	0	0	0	34,000	34,000
Dividends	0	0	0	(15,000)	(15,000)
Cash flow from financing activities (FCF)	11,000	21,000	52,000	34,000	34,000
Increase/decrease in cash (change in cash)	(5,000)	(16,000)	(1,000)	11,000	112,000
Beginning cash	25,000	20,000	4,000	3,000	3,000
Ending cash	$20,000	$4,000	$3,000	$14,000	$115,000

TABLE A1.3 Key Numbers

Key Numbers	Year 1	Year 2	Year 3	Year 4 Business as Usual	Year 4 Proactive/ Realistic
Cost of goods sold/sales	70.00%	69.33%	70.56%	70.48%	69.33%
Marketing, selling, general, admin exp/sales	31.00%	26.67%	26.00%	26.00%	26.00%
Net profit	$ (17,000)	$ 17,000	$ 13,000	$ 16,000	$ 28,000
Return on sales (ROS)	(3.40%)	2.27%	1.44%	1.52%	2.67%
Average assets	$237,000	$283,000	$347,500	$419,500	$425,500
Asset turnover	2.11	2.65	2.59	2.50	2.47
Return on assets (ROA)	(7.17%)	6.01%	3.74%	3.81%	6.58%
Average receivables	$ 15,000	$ 52,500	$ 92,500	$119,000	$ 96,000
Receivable turnover	33.33	14.29	9.73	8.82	10.94
Receivable days	11.0	25.6	37.5	41.4	33.4
Average inventory	$ 90,000	$120,000	$155,000	$189,500	$168,000
Inventory turnover	3.89	4.33	4.10	3.91	4.33
Inventory days	93.9	84.2	89.1	93.5	84.2
Average net fixed assets	$ 95,000	$ 85,000	$ 84,000	$ 91,000	$ 91,000
Net profit/net fixed assets	(17.89%)	20.00%	15.48%	17.58%	30.77%
Average equity	$196,500	$196,500	$211,500	$235,500	$241,500
Financial leverage	1.21	1.44	1.64	1.78	1.76
Return on equity (ROE)	(8.65%)	8.65%	6.15%	6.79%	11.59%

TABLE A1.4   Indirect Cash-Flow Statement

Indirect Cash-Flow Statement	Year 1	Year 2	Year 3	Year 4 Business as Usual	Year 4 Proactive/ Realistic
Net profit	($17,000)	$17,000	$13,000	$16,000	$28,000
Depreciation	10,000	10,000	12,000	14,000	14,000
Goodwill amortization	1,000	1,000	1,000	1,000	1,000
Change in receivables	(30,000)	(45,000)	(35,000)	(18,000)	28,000
Change in inventory	(30,000)	(30,000)	(40,000)	(29,000)	14,000
Change in payables	50,000	10,000	15,000	13,000	13,000
Change in taxes payable	0	0	1,000	0	0
Cash flow from operating activities (OCF)	(16,000)	(37,000)	(33,000)	(3,000)	98,000
Fixed asset investment	0	0	(20,000)	(20,000)	(20,000)
Other investments	0	0	0	0	0
Cash flow from investing activities (ICF)	0	0	(20,000)	(20,000)	(20,000)
Debt increases (decreases)	11,000	21,000	52,000	15,000	15,000
Stock sales (repurchases)	0	0	0	34,000	34,000
Dividends	0	0	0	(15,000)	(15,000)
Cash flow from financing activities (FCF)	11,000	21,000	52,000	34,000	34,000
Increase/decrease in cash (change in cash)	(5,000)	(16,000)	(1,000)	11,000	112,000
Beginning cash	25,000	20,000	4,000	3,000	3,000
Ending cash	$20,000	$4,000	$3,000	$14,000	$115,000

TABLE A1.5 Financial Scoreboard, SOHO Equipment, Year 1 ($000)ᵃ

Days: 365

Beginning Balance Sheet 12/31/00		Income Statement		Cash Statement		Ending Balance Sheet 12/31/01	
Cash	25			Cash Change	−5	Cash	20
Accounts Receivable	0	Sales	500	Collections (OCF)	470	Accounts Receivable	30
Inventory	75	Cost of Goods Sold	350	Inventory Paid (OCF)	380	Inventory	105
Other Operating Assets	0			Prepayments (OCF)	0	Other Operating Assets	0
Notes Receivable–Trade	0			Lend (Receive) (OCF)	0	Notes Receivable–Trade	0
Gross Fixed Assets	100			Fixed Asset Investment (ICF)	0	Gross Fixed Assets	100
Accumulated Depreciation	0	Depreciation+Amortization	10			Accumulated Depreciation	10
Net Fixed Assets	100					Net Fixed Assets	90
Other Investments	15	Intangible Amortization	1	Other Investment (ICF)	1	Other Investments	14
Total Assets	215					Total Assets	259
Accounts Payable	0	MSG&A Expense	155	Expense Paid (OCF)	105	Accounts Payable	50
Debt	10			Borrow (Payback) (FCF)	11	Debt	21
Other Operating Liabilities	0	Interest & Other Expenses	1	Interest & Other Paid (OCF)	1	Other Operating Liabilities	0
Income Tax Due	0	Income Tax Expense	0	Income Tax Paid (OCF)	0	Income Tax Due	0
Nonoperating Liabilities	0	Nonoperating Expense	0	NonoperatingExpPaid(FCF)	0	Nonoperating Liabilities	0
Stock	205			Paid In (FCF)	0	Stock	205
Retained Earnings	0	>>>Net Profit	−17	Dividend & Other (FCF)	−17	Retained Earnings	−17
Total Liabilities + Equity	215					Total Liabilities + Equity	259
		>>>Return on Assets	−7.17%	>>>Operating Cash Flow	−16		

ᵃ Financial Scoreboard/Mobley Matrix™ ©Compilation Copyright

(continues on page 164)

TABLE A1.6 Financial Performance Strategies, Year 1 ($000) (continued from page 163)

Net Profit / Sales		Sales / Average Assets		Net Profit / Average Assets		Average Assets / Average Equity		Net Profit / Average Equity
−3.40%		2.11		−7.17%		1.21		−8.65%
Return on Sales	×	Asset Turnover	=	Return on Assets	×	Financial Leverage	=	Return on Equity

Cost & Exp Info	(%)	Average Days & Other		Financial Statement Info		Cash-Flow Statement		>>>Three Bottom Lines	
COGS/Sales	70.00%	Receivables	11.0	Average Assets	237	Operating Cash Flow	−16	Operating Cash Flow (OCF)	−16
MSG&A Exp/Sales	31.00%	Inventory	93.9	Average Liabilities	41	Fixed Asset Investment	0	Net Profit (loss)	−17
Net Profit/Avg				Average Equity	197	Other Investing Cash Flow	0	Return on Assets (ROA)	−7.17%
Net Fixed Assets	−17.89%			Avg Net Fixed Assets	95	Financing Cash Flow	11		
						Change in Cash	−5		

Ending Balance Sheet
12/31/01

TABLE A1.7   Financial Scoreboard, SOHO Equipment, Year 2 ($000)[a]

Days: 365

Beginning Balance Sheet 12/31/01		Income Statement		Cash Statement		Ending Balance Sheet 12/31/02	
20	Cash			−16	Cash Change	4	Cash
30	Accounts Receivable	750	Sales	705	Collections (OCF)	75	Accounts Receivable
105	Inventory	520	Cost of Goods Sold	550	Inventory Paid (OCF)	135	Inventory
0	Other Operating Assets			0	Prepayments (OCF)	0	Other Operating Assets
0	Notes Receivable–Trade			0	Lend (Receive) (OCF)	0	Notes Receivable–Trade
100	Gross Fixed Assets			0	Fixed Asset Investment (ICF)	100	Gross Fixed Assets
10	Accumulated Depreciation	10	Depreciation+Amortization			20	Accumulated Depreciation
90	Net Fixed Assets					80	Net Fixed Assets
14	Other Investments	1	Intangible Amortization	1	Other Investment (ICF)	13	Other Investments
259	Total Assets					307	Total Assets
50	Accounts Payable	200	MSG&A Expense	190	Expense Paid (OCF)	60	Accounts Payable
21	Debt			21	Borrow (Payback) (FCF)	42	Debt
0	Other Operating Liabilities	2	Interest & Other Expenses	2	Interest & Other Paid (OCF)	0	Other Operating Liabilities
0	Income Tax Due	0	Income Tax Expense	0	Income Tax Paid (OCF)	0	Income Tax Due
0	Nonoperating Liabilities	0	Nonoperating Expense	0	NonoperatingExpPaid(FCF)	0	Nonoperating Liabilities
205	Stock			0	Paid In (FCF)	205	Stock
−17	Retained Earnings	17	>>>Net Profit	0	Dividend & Other (FCF)	0	Retained Earnings
259	Total Liabilities + Equity	6.01%	>>>Return on Assets	−37	>>>Operating Cash Flow	307	Total Liabilities + Equity

[a] Financial Scoreboard/Mobley Matrix™ ©Compilation Copyright

(continues on page 166)

TABLE A1.8   Financial Performance Strategies, Year 2 (continued from page 165)

$$\frac{\text{Net Profit}}{\text{Sales}} \;(2.27\%) \times \frac{\text{Sales}}{\text{Average Assets}} \;(2.65) = \frac{\text{Net Profit}}{\text{Average Assets}} \;(6.01\%) \times \frac{\text{Average Assets}}{\text{Average Equity}} \;(1.44) = \frac{\text{Net Profit}}{\text{Average Equity}} \;(8.65\%)$$

Return on Sales	Asset Turnover	Return on Assets	Financial Leverage	Return on Equity

Cost & Exp Info (%)

COGS/Sales	69.33%
MSG&A Exp/Sales	26.67%

Average Days & Other

Receivables	25.6
Inventory	84.2
Net Profit/Avg Net Fixed Assets	20.00%

Financial Statement Info

Average Assets	283
Average Liabilities	87
Average Equity	197
Avg Net Fixed Assets	85

Cash-Flow Statement

Operating Cash Flow	-37
Fixed Asset Investment	0
Other Investing Cash Flow	0
Financing Cash Flow	21
Change in Cash	-16

>>>Three Bottom Lines

Operating Cash Flow (OCF)	-37
Net Profit (loss)	17
Return on Assets (ROA)	6.01%

Ending Balance Sheet 12/31/02

TABLE A1.9 Financial Scoreboard SOHO Equipment, Year 3 ($000)ᵃ

Beginning Balance Sheet 12/31/02		Income Statement		Cash Statement		Ending Balance Sheet 12/31/03	
						Days:	365
Cash	4	Sales	900	Cash Change	−1	Cash	3
Accounts Receivable	75	Cost of Goods Sold	635	Collections (OCF)	865	Accounts Receivable	110
Inventory	135			Inventory Paid (OCF)	675	Inventory	175
Other Operating Assets	0			Prepayments (OCF)	0	Other Operating Assets	0
Notes Receivable–Trade	0			Lend (Receive) (OCF)	0	Notes Receivable–Trade	0
Gross Fixed Assets	100			Fixed Asset Investment (ICF)	20	Gross Fixed Assets	120
Accumulated Depreciation	20	Depreciation+Amortization	12			Accumulated Depreciation	32
Net Fixed Assets	80					Net Fixed Assets	88
Other Investments	13	Intangible Amortization	1	Other Investment (ICF)	1	Other Investments	12
Total Assets	307					Total Assets	388
Accounts Payable	60	MSG&A Expense	234	Expense Paid (OCF)	234	Accounts Payable	75
Debt	42			Borrow (Payback) (FCF)	52	Debt	94
Other Operating Liabilities	0	Interest & Other Expenses	4	Interest & Other Paid (OCF)	4	Other Operating Liabilities	0
Income Tax Due	0	Income Tax Expense	1	Income Tax Paid (OCF)	1	Income Tax Due	1
Nonoperating Liabilities	0	Nonoperating Expense	0	NonoperatingExpPaid(FCF)	0	Nonoperating Liabilities	0
Stock	205			Paid In (FCF)	0	Stock	205
Retained Earnings	0	>>>Net Profit	13	Dividend & Other (FCF)	0	Retained Earnings	13
Total Liabilities + Equity	307					Total Liabilities + Equity	388
		>>> Return on Assets	3.74%	>>>Operating Cash Flow	−33		

ᵃFinancial Scoreboard/Mobley Matrix™ ©Compilation Copyright

(continues on page 168)

TABLE A1.10 Financial Performance Strategies, Year 3 ($000) *(continued from page 167)*

Net Profit / Sales		Sales / Average Assets		Net Profit / Average Assets		Average Assets / Average Equity		Net Profit / Average Equity
1.44%		2.59		3.74%		1.64		6.15%
Return on Sales	×	Asset Turnover	=	Return on Assets	×	Financial Leverage	=	Return on Equity

Cost & Exp Info	*(%)*	*Average Days & Other*		*Financial Statement Info*		*Cash-Flow Statement*		*>>>Three Bottom Lines*	
COGS/Sales	70.56%	Receivables	37.5	Average Assets	348	Operating Cash Flow	−33	Operating Cash Flow (OCF)	−33
MSG&A Exp/Sales	26.00%	Inventory	89.1	Average Liabilities	136	Fixed Asset Investment	−20	Net Profit (loss)	13
		Net Profit/Avg Net Fixed Assets	15.48%	Average Equity	212	Other Investing Cash Flow	0	Return on Assets (ROA)	3.74%
				Avg Net Fixed Assets	84	Financing Cash Flow	52		
						Change in Cash	−1		

Ending Balance Sheet
12/31/03

TABLE A1.11 Financial Scoreboard SOHO Equipment, Year 4 ("business as usual")[a]

Days: 365

Beginning Balance Sheet 12/31/03		Income Statement		Cash Statement		Ending Balance Sheet 12/31/04	
Cash	3			Cash Change	11	Cash	14
Accounts Receivable	110	Sales	1050	Collections (OCF)	1032	Accounts Receivable	128
Inventory	175	Cost of Goods Sold	740	Inventory Paid (OCF)	769	Inventory	204
Other Operating Assets	0			Prepayments (OCF)	0	Other Operating Assets	0
Notes Receivable–Trade	0			Lend (Receive) (OCF)	0	Notes Receivable–Trade	0
Gross Fixed Assets	120			Fixed Asset Investment (ICF)	20	Gross Fixed Assets	140
Accumulated Depreciation	32	Depreciation+Amortization	14			Accumulated Depreciation	46
Net Fixed Assets	88					Net Fixed Assets	94
Other Investments	12	Intangible Amortization	1	Other Investment (ICF)	1	Other Investments	11
Total Assets	388					Total Assets	451
Accounts Payable	75	MSG&A Expense	273	Expense Paid (OCF)	260	Accounts Payable	88
Debt	94			Borrow (Payback) (FCF)	15	Debt	109
Other Operating Liabilities	0	Interest & Other Expenses	5	Interest & Other Paid (OCF)	5	Other Operating Liabilities	0
Income Tax Due	1	Income Tax Expense	1	Income Tax Paid (OCF)	1	Income Tax Due	1
Nonoperating Liabilities	0	Nonoperating Expense	0	NonoperatingExpPaid(FCF)	0	Nonoperating Liabilities	0
Stock	205			Paid In (FCF)	34	Stock	239
Retained Earnings	13	>>>Net Profit	16	Dividend & Other (FCF)	15	Retained Earnings	14
Total Liabilities + Equity	388	>>>Return on Assets	3.81%	>>>Operating Cash Flow	–3	Total Liabilities + Equity	451

(continues on page 170)

TABLE A1.12   Financial Performance Strategies, Year 4 ("business as usual") (continued from page 169)

Net Profit / Sales		Sales / Average Assets		Net Profit / Average Assets		Average Assets / Average Equity		Net Profit / Average Equity
1.52%		2.50		3.81%		1.78		6.79%
Return on Sales	×	Asset Turnover	=	Return on Assets	×	Financial Leverage	=	Return on Equity

Cost & Exp Info	(%)	Average Days & Other		Financial Statement Info		Cash-Flow Statement		>>>Three Bottom Lines	
COGS/Sales	70.48%	Receivables	41.4	Average Assets	420	Operating Cash Flow	−3	Operating Cash Flow (OCF)	−3
MSG&A Exp/Sales	26.00%	Inventory	93.5	Average Liabilities	184	Fixed Asset Investment	−20	Net Profit (loss)	16
		Net Profit/Avg Net Fixed Assets	17.58%	Average Equity	236	Other Investing Cash Flow	0	Return on Assets (ROA)	3.81%
				Avg Net Fixed Assets	91	Financing Cash Flow	34		
						Change in Cash	11		

Ending Balance Sheet 12/31/04

TABLE A1.11 Financial Scoreboard SOHO Equipment, Year 4 (proactive)[a]

Days: 365

Beginning Balance Sheet 12/31/03

Cash	3
Accounts Receivable	110
Inventory	175
Other Operating Assets	0
Notes Receivable–Trade	0
Gross Fixed Assets	120
Accumulated Depreciation	32
Net Fixed Assets	88
Other Investments	12
Total Assets	388
Accounts Payable	75
Debt	94
Other Operating Liabilities	0
Income Tax Due	1
Nonoperating Liabilities	0
Stock	205
Retained Earnings	13
Total Liabilities + Equity	388

Income Statement

Sales	1050
Cost of Goods Sold	728
Depreciation+Amortization	14
Intangible Amortization	1
MSG&A Expense	273
Interest & Other Expenses	5
Income Tax Expense	1
Nonoperating Expense	0
>>>Net Profit	28
>>>Return on Assets	6.58%

Cash Statement

Cash Change	112
Collections (OCF)	1078
Inventory Paid (OCF)	714
Prepayments (OCF)	0
Lend (Receive) (OCF)	0
Fixed Asset Investment (ICF)	20
Other Investment (ICF)	1
Expense Paid (OCF)	260
Borrow (Payback) (FCF)	15
Interest & Other Paid (OCF)	5
Income Tax Paid (OCF)	1
NonoperatingExpPaid(FCF)	0
Paid In (FCF)	34
Dividend & Other (FCF)	15
>>>Operating Cash Flow	98

Ending Balance Sheet 12/31/04

Cash	115
Accounts Receivable	82
Inventory	161
Other Operating Assets	0
Notes Receivable–Trade	0
Gross Fixed Assets	140
Accumulated Depreciation	46
Net Fixed Assets	94
Other Investments	11
Total Assets	463
Accounts Payable	88
Debt	109
Other Operating Liabilities	0
Income Tax Due	1
Nonoperating Liabilities	0
Stock	239
Retained Earnings	26
Total Liabilities + Equity	463

[a] Financial Scoreboard/Mobley Matrix™ ©Compilation Copyright

(continues on page 172)

TABLE A1.14 Financial Performance Strategies, Year 4 (proactive) (continued from page 171)

$\dfrac{\text{Net Profit}}{\text{Sales}}$		$\dfrac{\text{Sales}}{\text{Average Assets}}$		$\dfrac{\text{Net Profit}}{\text{Average Assets}}$		$\dfrac{\text{Average Assets}}{\text{Average Equity}}$		$\dfrac{\text{Net Profit}}{\text{Average Equity}}$
2.67%		2.47		6.58%		1.76		11.59%
Return on Sales	×	Asset Turnover	=	Return on Assets	×	Financial Leverage	=	Return on Equity

Cost & Exp Info	(%)	Average Days & Other		Financial Statement Info		Cash-Flow Statement		>>>Three Bottom Lines	
COGS/Sales	69.33%	Receivables	33.4	Average Assets	426	Operating Cash Flow	98	Operating Cash Flow (OCF)	98
MSG&A Exp/Sales	26.00%	Inventory	84.2	Average Liabilities	184	Fixed Asset Investment	–20	Net Profit (loss)	28
		Net Profit/Avg		Average Equity	242	Other Investing Cash Flow	0	Return on Assets (ROA)	6.58%
		Net Fixed Assets	30.77%	Avg Net Fixed Assets	91	Financing Cash Flow	34		
						Change in Cash	112		

Ending Balance Sheet
12/31/04

Appendix 2

Tips on Converting Your Company's Financials to the Financial Scoreboard

THE BASICS OF SETTING UP A FINANCIAL SCOREBOARD ARE explained in Chapter 6. And if your company's financials are as uncomplicated as SOHO Equipment's, the basics are all you need.

However, many companies have more complex financial statements, or they have line items that don't correspond exactly to the ones listed for our sample company. If that's the case, this Appendix will help you understand how to adapt your company's financials so that they fit into the Financial Scoreboard format.

REARRANGE LINE ITEMS

In the simplest case, all you'll have to do is reorganize the line items. First, get out your financial statements and compare them to the scoreboard on page 176 (Table A2.1). If your financials are more detailed, combine the items into the major headings listed on the sample. For example, sales commissions, office expenses, and advertising expenses may be listed separately, but they can all be combined into MSG&A.

Next, rearrange the line items so that the sequence on each one corresponds to the sequence on the Financial Scoreboard. The balance sheets and income statement shouldn't take much rearranging, but the cash-flow statement will need to be reorganized into the categories listed. Remember the logic explained in Chapter 4: you're classifying cash transactions according to whether they fit into operating cash flow (OCF), investing cash flow (ICF), or financing cash flow (FCF). Here's what each includes:

OCF = collections, inventory paid, prepayment, lending, expense paid, interest and other paid, income tax paid

ICF = fixed asset investment, other investment

FCF = borrowing, nonoperating expense paid, paid-in, dividends, and other

Naturally, you have to pay attention to the signs: a plus sign on any line item corresponds to a net inflow of cash, while a minus sign (parentheses) indicates a net outflow.

CREATE A DIRECT CASH-FLOW STATEMENT IF NECESSARY

If you have no cash-flow statement—or if you have only an indirect one—you can create a direct cash-flow statement using the Financial Scoreboard. Arrange your two balance sheets and income statement so that they correspond to the items on the scoreboard, and create a blank cash-flow statement with the categories found on the scoreboard. Then you can calculate the correct values according to the "horizontal math" by following the two rules mentioned in Chapter 6:

- Rule 1: For all cash-flow items *except* inventory paid, prepayments, lend, fixed-asset investment, other investment, borrow, and paid-in, use the following arithmetic: add the beginning balance sheet value to the income statement value, then subtract the ending balance sheet value.
- Rule 2: For the exceptions mentioned in rule 1, add the ending balance sheet value to the income statement value, then subtract the beginning balance sheet value.

Once you have created the cash-flow statement, double-check your arithmetic by doing "vertical math" to make sure your change in cash equals the difference between cash on the beginning balance sheet and cash on the ending balance sheet.

Compare your scoreboard to your company's prepared financials. Most of the time, the cash-flow numbers you calculate from the scoreboard will match the numbers that appear on your company's prepared financials. At times, however, there will be differences. For example, if you have sold fixed assets, if you have made business acquisitions, or if you have acquired fixed assets financed with payables or equity, you will find that the cash-flow figures don't match. They also won't match if you have made credit additions to inventory—that is, purchased inventory during the time span in question that has not yet been paid for.

How can this be? The answer is that some business transactions change the balance sheet but don't appear on either the income statement or the cash-flow statement. Say that your company buys $10,000 worth of inventory on December 15, but you don't pay for it until January. On December 31 you have all that additional inventory—yet no cash has changed hands. Your accountant will record the purchase into your journals and ledgers (probably as "credit additions to inventory"). He or she will also record an increase in payables of $10,000, thus fulfilling the requirements of double-entry bookkeeping. The income statement and cash statement will remain the same. The balance sheet will still balance, but it will look a little different.

To take account of this kind of transaction, Lou Mobley added one more vertical column to the matrix that we have christened the Financial Scoreboard. He called it balance sheet transfers. In this example, the credit addition to inventory appears on the same horizontal line as inventory, cost of goods sold, and inventory paid. Enter here the full year's inventory additions in credit additions to inventory $ not in inventory paid (see Table A2.1). When you're doing the horizontal math, it's a positive number because it represents inventory in, similar to inventory paid, whereas COGS represents inventory out. At the same time, an identical entry appears on the line with accounts payable, MSG&A, and expense paid. Enter here the full year's inventory additions in credit additions to inventory, and then increase expense paid by the same amount (see Table A2.1). It too is a positive number in doing the hori-

TABLE A2.1   Financial Scoreboard, SOHO Equipment, Year 3 ($000)[a]

Days: 365

Beginning Balance Sheet

Cash	4
Accounts Receivable	75
Inventory	135
Other Operating Assets	0
Notes Receivable–Trade	0
Gross Fixed Assets	100
Accumulated Depreciation	20
Net Fixed Assets	80
Other Investments	13
Total Assets	307
Accounts Payable	60
Debt	42
Other Operating Liabilities	0
Income Tax Due	0
Nonoperating Liabilities	0
Stock	205
Retained Earnings	0
Total Liabilities + Equity	307

Income Statement

Sales	900
Cost of Goods Sold	635
Depreciation+Amortization	12
Intangible Amortization	1
MSG&A Expense	234
Interest & Other Expenses	4
Income Tax Expense	1
Nonoperating Expense	0
>>>Net Profit	13
>>>Return on Assets	3.74%

Cash Statement

Cash Change	-1
Collections (OCF)	865
Inventory Paid (OCF)	0
Prepayments (OCF)	0
Lend (Receive) (OCF)	0
Fixed Asset Investment (ICF)	20
Other Investment (ICF)	1
Expense Paid (OCF)	894
Borrow (Payback) (FCF)	52
Interest & Other Paid (OCF)	4
Income Tax Paid (OCF)	1
NonoperatingExpPaid(FCF)	0
Paid In (FCF)	0
Dividend & Other (FCF)	13
>>>Operating Cash Flow	-33

Ending Balance Sheet

Cash	3
Accounts Receivable	110
Inventory	175
Other Operating Assets	0
Notes Receivable–Trade	0
Gross Fixed Assets	120
Accumulated Depreciation	32
Net Fixed Assets	88
Other Investments	12
Total Assets	388
Accounts Payable	75
Debt	94
Other Operating Liabilities	0
Income Tax Due	1
Nonoperating Liabilities	0
Stock	205
Retained Earnings	13
Total Liabilities + Equity	388

zontal math because it increases accounts payable. You wind up with an ending balance sheet showing the same amount of inventory and the same amount of payables.

There are other applications for balance sheet transfers as well. A stock dividend, for example, increases stock and decreases retained earnings but doesn't appear on the income statement or cash-flow statement. If your financial statements are complex (and most large companies' statements are extremely complex), you can delve into the footnotes and spot some relevant transactions—or, better, you just enter summary balance sheet transfer figures to make OCF, ICF, and FCF the same on the Financial Scoreboard as they are in your prepared financials. Usually the adjustments required are minor, but they must net out to the same change in cash.

Table A2.1 shows a complete Financial Scoreboard including balance sheet transfers.

PAYABLE DAYS

Balance sheet transfers have one other use: they let you calculate a ratio called payable days more precisely. Payable days is never a precise number, and the ratio is often of little use because small companies rarely have much leeway as to when they pay their bills. (If your payables are stretched out too far, chances are you don't need a ratio to tell you so!) However, here's how to calculate payable days for a one-year period:

$$\text{payable days} = \frac{\text{average payables} \times 365 \text{ days}}{\text{credit additions to inventory} + \text{MSG\&A}}$$

Average payables, of course, equals beginning payables plus ending payables divided by two. So for Year 3, average payables equaled $67,500, and multiplying this times 365 = $24,637,500. Credit additions to inventory equaled $675,000 and MSG&A expense equaled $234,000 for a combined total of $909,000. So for Year 3, payable days equaled $24,637,500 divided by $909,000 or 27.1 days. This means that in Year 3 it took the company approximately 27 days to pay suppliers, on average. Now if you are calculating the ratio for a month, you use thirty days in the numerator.

Appendix 3

Our (Nonsacred) Financial Glossary and Why You Need a Sacred One

ACCOUNTANTS AND FINANCIAL PEOPLE ARE NOTORIOUS FOR using different terminology for the same concepts or items on a financial statement. Should the top line on an income statement be labeled "sales" or "revenues"? Is the income statement itself called that—or is it the "profit-and-loss statement" or "statement of operations"? Is the bottom line on that statement (whatever you name it) called "profit after tax" or "net profit" or "net earnings" or "net income"?

And if you really want to start a debate, just ask a roomful of accountants to define the term "free cash flow." You could come back in a few days and the arguments wouldn't be over.

We can't change this fact. But we do urge you to adopt *one* set of terms for your own company and never deviate from it. Pick a word for the bottom line on an income statement—we happen to like "net profit," but you can choose whatever you like—and *stick to it.* Always use that term to refer to that line item. Do the same thing with all the other line items on the financial statements. If your balance sheet contains the entry "net property, plant, and equipment"—and if you like that term—then remember that this is the same as "net fixed assets" but don't *call* the item net fixed assets. Call it net property, plant, and equipment. Always!

Why? Financial statements and financial terminology are complicated enough. People get confused when there's no need. Just pick one set of terms and stick to it. When you communicate with your accountant, your managers, and your employees, use your *sacred financial glossary* and never deviate from it. It will make communication much clearer and hence much easier.

For handy reference, here is a glossary of the terms used in this book, plus many of the most common synonyms.

Accounts payable. Line item on a **balance sheet.** Amount a company owes to vendors and suppliers.

Accounts receivable. Line item on a **balance sheet.** Amount a company is owed by customers.

Accrual. Principle governing most business accounting, including the preparation of **balance sheets** and most **income statements.** Under the principle of accrual, **sales** are recorded when they are earned—that is, when goods or services are provided—rather than when the cash for the sales actually changes hands. Similarly, **expenses** are recorded when they are incurred, rather than when they are settled. (A so-called cash-based income statement does not use the principle of accrual; it records sales and expenses only when cash changes hands. See Chapter 3 for a discussion.)

Amortization. Line item on an **income statement.** An expense reducing earnings, theoretically reflecting the declining value of a company's intangible assets during the time span covered by the statement. Somewhat similar to **depreciation.**

Asset turnover. Sales divided by **average assets.** A measure of a company's effectiveness in generating sales from a given level of assets. Also known as marketing leverage.

Assets. Left-hand or top portion of the **balance sheet.** Assets are items of future value, tangible and intangible, used by a business. The most important assets on most companies' balance sheets are **cash, accounts receivable, inventory,** and **fixed assets.** Assets are generally valued at the amount of money a company has spent so far in acquiring the asset.

Assets, average. The average value of a company's **assets** during a given span of time, calculated by adding assets at the beginning of that time span and assets at the end of the time span and dividing by two.

Assets, fixed. Tangible items of value, such as buildings, vehicles, and machinery, to be used in a company's business in the future. Also known as **property, plant,** and **equipment.**

Assets, intangible. Items of value other than **cash, accounts receivable, inventory,** and **fixed assets.** Examples include patents and **goodwill.**

Assets-to-equity ratio. Total **assets** divided by total **equity.** Since a higher assets-to-equity ratio indicates relatively higher **liabilities,** this ratio measures a company's use of (and possible dependence on) creditors' money. Also known as financial leverage or the equity multiplier.

Balance sheet. One of the three key financial statements used to indicate a company's financial performance. The balance sheet is a "snapshot" at a given point in time and always shows a company's **assets, liabilities,** and **equity.** Also known as statement of financial position.

Cash. Line item on a **balance sheet** representing amounts held in currency or readily available bank deposits (including petty cash, checking accounts, and money market funds).

Cash equivalents. Line item on a **balance sheet** representing amounts held in short-term certificates of deposit or other instruments that are readily convertible into **cash.**

Cash flow from financing activities. See **Financing cash flow.**

Cash flow from investing activities. See **Investing cash flow.**

Cash flow from operating activities. See **Operating cash flow.**

Cash Flow. All additions to, and subtractions from, a company's holdings of **cash** during a given time period.

Cash-flow statement, direct. One of the three key financial statements used to indicate a company's financial performance. A *direct* cash-flow statement summarizes and categorizes all transactions according to their cash impact during a given time period.

Cash-flow statement, indirect. A common alternative to a **direct cash-flow statement.** An *indirect* cash-flow statement has many similarities to a direct cash-flow statement, but instead of focusing exclusively on cash inflows and outflows, it reconciles **net profit** to **operating cash flow** according to accounting rules.

Change in cash. Line item on a **cash-flow statement** indicating a company's net increase or decrease in **cash** during a given time period.

Collections. Line item on a **direct cash-flow statement** indicating a company's inflows of cash from settlement of **accounts receivable** during a given time period.

Common stock. Line item on a **balance sheet** indicating amount invested by a company's shareholders to buy common stock from the company. (This item can be reduced if the company buys stock back from stockholders.)

Cost of goods sold (COGS). Line item on an **income statement** showing costs associated with providing all goods sold during a given time period. COGS in a manufacturing company typically includes the cost of materials and direct labor involved in producing a product, plus a portion of **manufacturing overhead** attributed to the products sold. COGS in a wholesale or retail company typically includes the cost of goods purchased for resale, plus shipping charges associated with acquiring the goods ("freight in"), but only for the products sold during the period.

Cost of sales, cost of services (COS). Line item on the **income statement** of many service companies indicating costs specifically associated with the provision of a service to customers.

Current assets. Line item on a **balance sheet** indicating **assets** that are expected to be converted into cash in 365 days or less. Current assets includes **cash** and **cash equivalents**, **accounts receivable**, **inventory**, and other current assets (such as prepaid expense and most deposits).

Current liabilities. Line item on a **balance sheet** indicating **liabilities** that are expected to reduce **cash** within 365 days.

Current ratio. **Current assets** divided by **current liabilities**. A common measure of a company's **liquidity**, especially important to creditors.

Days sales outstanding (DSO). See **Receivable days.**

Debt. Line item on a **balance sheet** indicating outstanding principal owed on a company's interest-bearing loans.

Debt-to-equity ratio. Total **debt** divided by total **equity**. One measure of a company's **solvency**, especially important to lenders.

Depreciation, accumulated. Line item on a **balance sheet** reflecting the total depreciation expensed between the date a **fixed asset** was purchased and the date of the balance sheet, for all fixed assets a company still possesses. **Gross fixed assets** minus accumulated depreciation equals net fixed assets.

Depreciation. Line item on an **income statement.** An expense reducing earnings, theoretically reflecting the declining value of a company's **fixed assets** during the time period covered by the statement. A fixed asset is depreciated over its useful life according to various accounting rules.

Dividends. Line item on a **cash-flow statement** indicating earnings distributed to a company's shareholders by virtue of their share ownership.

Du Pont equation. Mathematical expression showing the relationship between **return on sales, asset turnover, return on assets, financial leverage,** and **return on equity.** (See pages 109–117.)

EBITDA. Acronym for earnings before interest, taxes, **depreciation,** and **amortization.** A profit subtotal that can be derived from the **income statement,** tracked by certain industries such as the telecommunications industry.

Equity. Line item on a **balance sheet** indicating claims on a company's assets held by the company's shareholders. According to the basic accounting equation, equity equals **assets** minus **liabilities.**

Equity, average. The average value of a company's equity during a given period, calculated by adding **equity** at the beginning of that time span and equity at the end of the time span and dividing by two.

Equity multiplier. See **Assets-to-equity ratio.**

Expenses. A category that often appears on an **income statement,** including marketing, selling, general, and administrative expenses incurred during the time period covered. Expenses does not include costs specifically related to providing products or services, which are totaled instead under **cost of goods sold** or **cost of services.**

Financial leverage. See **Assets-to-equity ratio.**

Financial Scoreboard. Matrix developed by the late Lou Mobley of IBM Corp. indicating line-item relationships between a company's beginning **balance sheet, income statement, cash-flow statement,** and ending **balance sheet.** Also known as the Mobley Matrix™ (trademark owned by Mobley Matrix International, Inc.).

Financing cash flow (FCF). Also known as cash flow from financing activities. Grouping of line items on a **cash-flow statement** reflecting inflows and outflows of cash related to borrowing and payback of loans (principal only), purchase or sale of stock, and dividends.

Finished goods. Portion of a company's **inventory** that is currently available for sale.

Fixed asset investment. Line item on a **cash-flow statement** reflecting inflows and outflows of cash related to purchase or sale of **fixed assets**. Also known as capital expenditure.

Free cash flow. Measure of cash flow sometimes calculated as **operating cash flow** minus **fixed asset investment.** This is a measure not clearly available on a CPA-audited **cash-flow statement.** This measure may be calculated in other ways by other financial professionals.

General and administrative (G&A). Grouping of line items on an **income statement** reflecting **expenses** (such as office rent, office utilities, and salaries of office personnel) not directly related to the provision of goods and services.

Generally accepted accounting principles (GAAP). Code of rules followed by certified public accountants (CPAs) in the preparation and audit of a business's financial statements.

Goodwill. Line item on the **balance sheet** indicating one type of **intangible asset.** Goodwill is established when a company purchases another company's **assets** for a price greater than the actual value of identifiable assets. The difference is goodwill, which is considered to be the amount the purchaser is paying for client lists, covenants not to compete, processes, technology, and other intangible items of value. Goodwill must be amortized over its estimated future life.

Gross fixed assets. Line item on a **balance sheet** reflecting the historical cost of **fixed assets** still owned by a company.

Gross profit. Line item on an **income statement** indicating the difference between sales and **cost of goods sold.** (Typically, gross profit is the net after subtracting manufacturing depreciation.)

Income statement. One of the three key financial statements used to indicate a company's financial performance. An income statement indicates a company's **sales** and **expenses** (including **cost of goods sold**

where relevant) and shows the difference between them as **net profit.**
Also known as profit-and-loss statement, P&L, statement of operations,
and statement of earnings.

Inventory. Line item on a balance sheet indicating the cost value of
raw materials, work in process, and **finished goods** available for sale.
Inventory can be valued according to various accounting principles, but
not at market value until it is sold.

Inventory, average. Average value of a company's inventory during a
given time span, calculated by adding beginning inventory and ending
inventory and dividing by two.

Inventory days. Average number of days in a given period between
purchase of a product (or **raw materials**) and sale of a product. (This
definition is simplified for ease of use.) Inventory days is equal to the
number of days in the period divided by **inventory turnover.**

Inventory paid. Line item on a **cash-flow statement** indicating
amounts spent on purchase of goods for **inventory.**

Inventory turnover. Measure of how quickly a company "turns over"
its inventory. Inventory turnover for a given period is calculated by
taking **cost of goods sold** for that period and dividing by **average inventory.**

Investing cash flow (ICF). Also known as cash flow from investing
activities. Grouping of line items on a **cash-flow statement** reflecting inflows and outflows of cash related to purchase or sale of **fixed assets** and
other investments.

Liabilities. First part of right-hand or lower portion of the **balance
sheet** (depending on balance sheet format). Liabilities are claims on a
company's **assets** held by creditors.

Liquidity. A company's ability to settle its current liabilities with current assets.

Marketing leverage. See **Asset turnover.**

Marketing, selling, general, and administrative (MSG&A). Grouping of line items on an **income statement** reflecting **expenses** not specifically related to providing goods or services and therefore not included
in **cost of goods sold.** Also known as **overhead** or (in manufacturing
companies) nonmanufacturing overhead.

Matching principle. The accounting principle of **accrual** stating that costs and **expenses** recorded on an **income statement** shall be linked, or matched, to sales recorded during the time span covered by the statement. This principle is intended to help determine if a company is making money on products or services sold during the time span.

Mobley Matrix™. See **Financial Scoreboard.**

Net cash provided by financing activities. See **Financing cash flow.**

Net cash provided by investing activities. See **Investing cash flow.**

Net cash provided by operating activities. See **Operating cash flow.**

Net fixed assets. Line item on a **balance sheet** indicating **gross fixed assets** minus accumulated **depreciation.** Also known as net book value.

Net profit. Line item on an **income statement** indicating the difference between **sales** and all costs and **expenses,** including noncash charges such as **depreciation.** One of the three key measures of a company's performance.

Notes receivable–trade. Line item on a **balance sheet** indicating outstanding principal on interest-bearing loans owed to a company, resulting from sale of products or services.

Operating cash flow (OCF). Also known as cash flow from operating activities. Grouping of line items on a **cash-flow statement** reflecting inflows and outflows of cash related to the ongoing business of a company. Operating cash flow excludes inflows or outflows related to **fixed asset investment,** other investment, borrowing and payback of loans, purchase or sale of stock, and dividends. One of the three key measures of a company's performance.

Operating income. Line item on many companies' **income statements.** Operating income is **sales** minus **cost of goods sold** minus **marketing, selling, general and administrative expenses** minus **depreciation** and **amortization.** Also known as operating profit. (Caution: this term may be defined in other ways by other financial professionals).

Operating profit. See **Operating income.**

Overhead, manufacturing. For manufacturing companies, indirect manufacturing costs included in **cost of goods sold,** such as supervisory payroll, maintenance supplies, and factory utilities.

Overhead, nonmanufacturing. See **Marketing, selling, general, and administrative expenses.**

Owners' equity. See **Equity.**

P&L. See **Income statement.**

Paid-in capital. Line item on a **balance sheet** indicating amounts invested in a company by its shareholders over and above par value of company stock. (Since common stock frequently has no par value, paid-in capital is not always listed on a balance sheet.)

Payable days. Measure of average time a company requires to settle outstanding **accounts payable** during a given time span. Payable days is equal to average payables times the number of days in the period, divided by the sum of credit additions to inventory plus MSG&A.

Payables. See **Accounts payable.**

Profit after tax. See **Net profit.**

Profit margin. See **Return on sales (ROS).**

Profit. See **Net profit; Operating income; EBITDA; Gross profit.**

Profit-and-loss statement. See **Income statement.**

Property, plant, and equipment. See **Assets, fixed.**

Quick ratio. A measure of a company's **liquidity.** The quick ratio is calculated by adding a company's **cash** and **accounts receivable,** then dividing by the sum of **accounts payable** and other **current liabilities.**

Raw materials. Portion of a company's **inventory** consisting of unprocessed materials that will be used in the future production of goods.

Receivable days. Measure of average time a company requires to collect **accounts receivable** during a given time span. Receivable days is calculated by dividing the number of days in the time span by **receivable turnover.**

Receivable turnover. Measure of how quickly a company "turns over" its **accounts receivable.** Receivable turnover for a given time span is calculated by taking **sales** for that time span and dividing by **average receivables.**

Receivables, average. The average value of a company's **accounts receivable** during a given span of time, calculated by adding accounts receivable at the beginning of that time span and accounts receivable at the end of the time span and dividing by two.

Receivables. See **Accounts receivable.**

Retained earnings. Line item on a **balance sheet** indicating accumulated **net profit** earned by a company not yet paid out in **dividends** since the beginning of a company's life. (This line item may be reduced by the stock a company buys back from its shareholders.)

Return on assets (ROA). Net profit divided by **average assets.** One of the three key measures of a company's performance, return on assets measures a company's effectiveness in generating profit from a given level of assets.

Return on equity (ROE). Net profit divided by **average equity.** Return on equity measures a company's effectiveness in generating profit from a given level of shareholder investment.

Return on sales (ROS). Net profit divided by **sales.** Return on sales measures a company's efficiency in generating profit from a given level of sales. Also known as net margin, net profit margin, or profit margin.

Revenue. See **Sales.**

Sales. First line item on an **income statement.** Indicates the total sales value of goods and services provided to customers during a given time span. Also known as revenue.

Solvency. Measure of a company's ability to function as an ongoing business. One measure of solvency is whether **assets** exceed **liabilities.**

Statement of earnings. See **Income statement.**

Statement of financial position. See **Balance sheet.**

Statement of operations. See **Income statement.**

Stock. Line item on **Financial Scoreboard** that equals total **equity** minus **retained earnings.** (This line includes all **common stock** plus paid-in capital.)

Taxes payable. Line item on a **balance sheet** indicating amount owed to governments for income taxes.

Work in process (WIP). Portion of a company's **inventory** consisting of goods not yet finished and available for sale; WIP includes materials, direct labor, and manufacturing overhead (raw materials are excluded).

Appendix 4

A Guide to Ratios

$$\text{Average assets} = \frac{\text{beginning assets} + \text{ending assets}}{2}$$

$$\text{Average equity} = \frac{\text{beginning equity} + \text{ending equity}}{2}$$

$$\text{Average inventory} = \frac{\text{beginning inventory} + \text{ending inventory}}{2}$$

$$\text{Average net fixed assets} = \frac{\text{beginning net fixed assets} + \text{ending net fixed assets}}{2}$$

$$\text{Average receivables} = \frac{\text{beginning receivables} + \text{ending receivables}}{2}$$

$$\text{Assets-to-equity ratio} = \frac{\text{total assets}}{\text{total equity}}$$

$$\text{Asset turnover (1 yr.)} = \frac{\text{sales}}{\text{average assets}}$$

$$\text{COGS as percentage of sales} = \frac{\text{COGS} \times 100}{\text{sales}}$$

$$\text{Current ratio} = \frac{\text{cash} + \text{accounts receivable} + \text{inventory} + \text{other current assets}}{\text{accounts payable} + \text{other current liabilities}}$$

$$\text{Debt-to-equity ratio} = \frac{\text{debt}}{\text{equity}}$$

$$\text{Equity multiplier or financial leverage} = \frac{\text{assets}}{\text{equity}}$$

$$\text{Inventory days (1 yr.)} = \frac{\text{average inventory} \times 365 \text{ days}}{\text{COGS}}$$

OR

$$\frac{365 \text{ days}}{\text{inventory turnover}}$$

$$\text{Inventory turnover (1 yr.)} = \frac{\text{cost of goods sold}}{\text{average inventory}}$$

$$\text{MSG\&A as percentage of sales} = \frac{\text{MSG\&A} \times 100}{\text{sales}}$$

$$\text{Quick ratio} = \frac{\text{cash} + \text{accounts receivable}}{\text{accounts payable} + \text{other current liabilities}}$$

$$\text{Receivable days (1 yr.)} = \frac{\text{average receivables} \times 365 \text{ days}}{\text{sales}}$$

OR

$$\frac{365 \text{ days}}{\text{receivable turnover}}$$

$$\text{Receivable turnover (1 yr.)} = \frac{\text{sales}}{\text{average receivables}}$$

$$\text{Return on assets (1 yr.)} = \frac{\text{net profit}}{\text{average assets}}$$

$$\text{Return on equity (1 yr.)} = \frac{\text{net profit}}{\text{average equity}}$$

$$\text{Return on sales} = \frac{\text{net profit}}{\text{sales}}$$

Note: For all items listed "1 yr.," it is possible to calculate the ratio for shorter periods, such as monthly, provided the calculation is then adjusted to an annual calculation. For example, return on assets for one month is net profit for the month multiplied by twelve, then divided by average assets for the month being tracked.

Appendix 5

A History of the Mobley Matrix

BY LOUIS B. MOBLEY

I developed the Mobley Matrix over a 27-year period starting in 1956. That was the year IBM started its Executive School to develop its executives by means of a one-week, live-in intensive program at Sands Point, N.Y., near New York City. When middle managers moved into the executive ranks of IBM's domestic and foreign organization, they were all scheduled for the Executive School.

The program was quite successful. But the unit on finance was the most difficult to teach. Professors from the business schools were helpful, but their accounting language and focus on company problems tended to distract the executive students from a clear understanding of finance.

The use of computers to play management games was the most helpful teaching aid, but the financial relationships were in the program of the computer and were no more visible to the student than the mysterious financial data seen in real life.

When I became director of the school, in 1959, I was challenged to find a way to make finance teachable. My first task was to really understand it myself. Fortunately, I could hire the "experts" to come in as resource leaders in the school. I had my list of questions to ask them. Slowly I began to understand. One myth after another had to be washed from my mind.

The most serious myth I held was reading cash into the income statement. Since those figures had dollar marks beside them, I thought sales were dollars that flowed into the company during the period shown by the income statement. Not so. Sales measured the billings, not the collections. I learned that cost of goods sold (COGS) was not what was spent to acquire inventory during the period depicted by the income statement; rather, it was an allocation of prior cash outlays for inventory charged to the current period and corresponding to sales for the current period.

Depreciation was the toughest of all. The accountants explained depreciation as a non-cash charge to income which is an internal generator of cash. "What kind of double-talk is that?" I asked. Much later, I discovered that depreciation, like COGS, is merely an allocation of a prior cash outlay for plant or equipment to the current income period. I discovered that a cash outlay for a fixed asset must be charged as a cost of doing business in each of a series of years covering the useful life of the asset. This annual charge is called depreciation.

To my amazement, cash outlays for things like organization expense, research and development, and even marketing expense could sometimes be "capitalized"—that is, put on the balance sheet and charged against income in future accounting periods by an entry on the income statement called amortization.

I finally realized that the income statement had no cash in it. It was a measure of commitments requiring future cash inflows and outlays, or amortizations of previous cash outlays. Net income (which nets out all these commitments and amortizations) was the non-cash measure of company performance. Many of the non-cash items on the income statement are related to cash outlays in other periods of time (past and future), and are not accurate measures of current value with inflation.

The professors I brought in from the business schools to lead strategy cases were the most helpful. Strategy cases were very instructive. They typically have many pages of verbal information about the company, but only one page of financial data. Typically, this financial data showed historical income statements and balance sheets. Most students skipped this page. The company could be making big profits but was out of cash. How could that be? I wondered. How could we know what was going on cash-wise if there is no cash in the income statement? One professor explained it simply:

If a company's accounts receivable increases by a thousand dollars, then it sold a thousand dollars more than it collected. Merely subtract a thousand dollars from the sales income figure and you know collections. Do the same for any other balance sheet account.

This was an "a-ha" experience to me. Now, I knew how to connect income statements to balance sheets. The cash statement was the connecting link!

The relationship became clear. Starting balance sheet, plus or minus income data, plus or minus cash data equals ending balance sheet. It remained only for me to insert the whole income statement and the whole cash statement between the two balance sheets. The matrix was born.

By using the matrix, I found that finances could finally be taught to nonfinancial executives so they can communicate well with financial executives. It was a useful tool for salesmen to size up prospective companies. IBM executives named it "The Mobley Matrix."

When I retired from IBM in 1970, I created a matrix for my own company, Mobley and Associates. Each quarter I created my cash-flow statement as I reconciled my bank statement, entered the income data, then calculated the next balance sheet.

My small-business clients frequently use the matrix for their own accounting. They first enter cash summaries, by account, to develop a cash-flow statement for the period. They then apply the usual procedures to develop the income statement for the same period, and then use both of these to carry forward the balance sheet to the next period. Their accountants love the precision, and communication between parties is simplified because the matrix cuts through the prevailing myth and ignorance about these crucial measures and relationships.

My nonprofit clients—and even individuals who keep income and expense records as well as balance sheets—are surprised to learn they also have an income statement, to the extent that they have accruals and amortizations of a non-cash nature. Just as for-profit businesses find it necessary to move to cash-flow figures, associations, churches, schools, and other nonprofit organizations should learn to use the income statement (profit and loss statement).

All organizations need both the cash statement and the non-cash statements to evaluate their performance. The balance sheet glues the two together at specified intervals to show the end result of both the cash dimension and the non-cash dimension of all transactions. Perhaps the greatest value to be derived by publishing the financial data of any organization, profit or nonprofit, in this matrix format is the prospect that financial reports will begin to be read and understood.

(This is an excerpt from the Mobley Matrix[R] software manual, the rights to which were purchased by Chuck Kremer from Lou Mobley in 1983. It is reproduced here with permission of Lou's son Chris Mobley.)

About the Authors

Chuck Kremer, CPA, has many years of experience as an accountant, a corporate controller, and a business consultant. His expertise is in helping companies successfully convert financial literacy into winning performance. A regular presenter at MIT and *Inc.* magazine seminars, Chuck has written articles for the *Journal of Accountancy* and *Management Accounting* magazines.

Chuck is also a senior business literacy consultant at Educational Discoveries, Inc. (EDI), a strategic learning solutions and organizational design company (and a Provant company) in Boulder, Colorado. He cocreated and presents EDI's Financial Game for Decision Making, a course for nonfinancial decisionmakers through which thousands of people have enjoyed learning financial concepts by running the Real Good Lemonade Company. He also presents EDI's *The Accounting Game™*, the most successful financial program for nonfinancial people in the world, which teaches accounting by having students run a child's lemonade stand. Both programs are part of EDI's Financial Literacy Advantage, which provides customized learning, consulting, and implementation tools.

Ron Rizzuto, Ph.D., is professor of finance at Daniels College of Business, University of Denver. He has published numerous articles on a variety of topics, including capital expenditure analysis, mergers and acquisitions, and corporate financial planning. Ron cofounded the University of Denver's entrepreneurship program and has won several awards for his teaching. He also has an extensive background in executive education and has designed in-house training programs and conferences for clients such as Time Warner Cable, TCI Communications, and US West. Ron holds a B.S. in finance from the University of Colorado and an M.B.A. and a Ph.D. (in finance and economics) from New York University. He has also coauthored *Friendly Finance, Finally: A Total Systems Approach to Business Finance*, with Chuck Kremer and Kate McKeown.

John Case is an executive editor at Harvard Business School Publishing, where he edits the monthly newsletter *Harvard Management Update*. A veteran business journalist, he was a senior writer at *Inc.* magazine for many years and is a nationally known expert on open-book management. John is author of five books, including *Open-Book Management* (HarperBusiness, 1995) and *The Open-Book Experience* (Addison-Wesley, 1998).